C000216600

Bound To Be Free:
home-based education as a positive alternative to paying the hidden costs of 'free' education

by Jan Fortune-Wood

Educational Heretics Press

Published 2001 by Educational Heretics Press
113 Arundel Drive, Bramcote Hills, Nottingham NG9 3FQ

British Cataloguing in Publication Data

Fortune-Wood, Jan
       Bound to be free: home-based education as a positive
       alternative to paying the hidden costs of 'free' education
       1.home-schooling 2.Education – Moral and ethical
       aspects
       I.Title
       371'.042

ISBN   1-900219-20-4

Design and production: Educational Heretics Press

Cover design by John Haxby, Edinburgh EH6 6QH

Printed by Mastaprint Plus Ltd. (telephone 0115 939 1772)

And a woman who held a babe against her bosom said, "Speak to us of Children."

And he said:

Your children are not your children.

They are the sons and daughters of Life's longing for itself.

They come through you but not from you,

And though they are with you, yet they belong not to you.

You may give them your love but not your thoughts.

For they have their own thoughts.

You may house their bodies but not their souls,

For their souls dwell in the house of tomorrow, which you cannot visit, not even in your dreams.

You may strive to be like them, but seek not to make them like you.

For life goes not backward nor tarries with yesterday. ...

(Kahlil Gibran: *The Prophet*, Wordsworth Editions Ltd. Nov 1996)

Contents

Acknowledgements

A lot of people have supported the writing of this book. Many thanks are due to Roland and Janet Meighan for their practical support and valuable input. Enormous thanks are due to my family who are always supportive of my projects and show endless patience. The adventure of home-education is one I share with them and it is a constant delight and privilege.

Two people have done an enormous amount to assist with this book, not only proof reading, but also commenting on the text, offering valuable criticism and generously giving me their time and insight. I would like to dedicate this book to Sue Cvach and Peter Tuffnell with thanks.

Thanks are due to many people who helped with this book, whether directly or through inspiration. Thank you to Roland Meighan, who has remained supportive throughout this project. Thanks to Martine Archer and Sue Cvach, who proof-read the text for me with meticulous care. Thank you to Peter Tuffnell and Sue Cvach, who read my drafts and made valuable comments and suggestions.

Two special thanks remain. The first is to the *Taking Children Seriously* (TCS) community, those people who write on the Internet list and in the journal, and who have helped me make the journey this far in taking children seriously. It has been an enormous and life changing journey and I have needed, been given, and continue to be given, an enormous amount of support on the way. Thank you to all who have been involved and who go on supporting this radical and wonderful alternative. Most especially thanks to Sarah Lawrence for her support, clear thinking, humour and persistence.

Secondly, an enormous thanks to my family, my husband Mike and our four children. Finding and implementing *Taking Children Seriously* in our lives has been a difficult and richly rewarding experience. Together, we know that we have a very long way to go still and we are very aware of how fallible we are and how often we get things wrong. Despite our short-comings we are optimistic. We know that neither guilt nor defeatism are useful alternatives. Thanks are due to them for making this journey with me.

Jan Fortune-Wood

Introduction

My book *Doing it their way* considers the primacy of intrinsic motivation in autonomous learning, and contends that the unimpeded growth of knowledge requires both an increased definition of education and an abandonment of coercive parenting practices. *Without Boundaries,* my second book, expands on this latter theme, arguing that both in theory and in practice, coercion is not only destructive of personal autonomy, but inimical to learning and the growth of knowledge. In this third book, *Bound to be Free* I will explore the myth that compulsory, state-provided education is free education and look at the impact this provision has on our freedom and autonomy, as children, parents or society.

The rhetoric of a state-provided education system, which is free at the point of access and funded by taxation, has become almost universally accepted as the most economically efficient and the most socially equitable means of delivering high quality education to as many children as possible. It is not the remit of this book to become embroiled in questions of whether the state should provide education for children whose parents are either unable or unwilling to take on this responsibility for them. The growth of alternatives, however, particularly the rapid growth of home education across all sections of society, does raise fundamental questions. The two considered in this book are: if schooling is provided by the state, whose interests does it serve? And, is 'free' schooling really free, or does the apparent freedom mask a range of hidden costs over which consumers of education have little control?

The book is divided into six chapters. The introductory chapter sets out the thesis that 'free' compulsory education is a myth, which hides a whole range of 'costs': namely, **financial** costs; **social** costs; **emotional** costs; and **skill** costs. For autonomy and true freedom in education to flourish, we need to look to the DIY approach of home education, whether undertaken by individual families or by voluntary communities.

The next four chapters will draw on specific themes from this overview to examine them in more detail. In chapter two, **'Nothing is Free'**, I will consider how the myth of 'free' education focuses the responsibility and accountability for education in state machinery, and contend that since financial control and philosophical control inevitably go hand in hand, parents must take back the former if they value the latter. In chapter three, **'The myth of what's best**

for you', I will examine the **social** costs of free compulsory education, including the rise of medical, psychological and civil liberty intervention into families under the guise of education. I will look at how non-educational welfare concerns have become accepted as educational concerns and show how such welfare concerns are not the proper territory of education, and why welfare and education must be seen as discrete issues in terms of approaches to home education.

In chapter four, **'The cost of conformity'**, I will consider the cost to individuals of being required to conform to institutionalised systems. I will consider the **emotional** costs of bullying and labeling and argue that the resulting attack on individuality and coercion damage is inimical to free society and a tragic waste of human resources. I will go on, in chapter five, **'Resources, not experts'**, to examine the **skill** costs of free education. I will focus on how parents and children are de-skilled in favour of 'experts', and propose that both philosophically and pragmatically, as we move into an event-driven, post-modern society, such de-skilling is an inappropriate outcome for education and must be replaced by a culture of mentors and resources.

Finally, I will propose that for autonomy and true freedom in education to flourish, we need to look to the Do-It-Yourself positive alternative of home education, whether undertaken by individual families or by voluntary communities. I will look at the alternative and positive 'costs' of home education with emphasis on retaining philosophical control and personal accountability; retaining choice over the content of education; building an educational culture which respects civil liberties; promoting divergence, individuality and emotional health; focusing the skills base in families; transforming a culture of experts to a culture of resources. I will argue that home education models a system that leads the way in event-driven, flexible, modern living and learning and has the potential to promote autonomy and freedom in education.

A note on memes

During the course of this book you will find certain concepts and theories referred to as memes. The term was first coined by Richard Dawkins to describe theories that function within culture in a way that is analogous to the functioning of genes within the human body. In other words they are self-replicating ideas or sometimes clusters of self-replicating ideas (memeplexes) which have served a purpose which has given them particular status as 'truths' or self apparent. That is not to say that memes are necessarily true or that they determine us. It is simply that there are ideas that have become, for complex cultural and evolutionary reasons, deeply entrenched theories. *The Taking Children Seriously* (TCS) website describes memes as replicators and goes on,

> "Whether something is a meme or not depends on how it is transmitted, not on its content per se. So, for example, shyness or fear of making a fool of oneself, are not, in general, memes because they suggest coercion-induced irrationality rather than ideas which might be replicators. The coercive parenting ideas that led to the shyness or fear of making a fool of oneself might well be replicators though. And if that fear plays a role in causing the parents to hold those ideas and coerce their children in a way that makes them acquire the same fear, then the fear itself is part of the meme.

> "Whenever parents behave in ways that cause their children to grow up behaving in ways that cause their children to grow up to cause the very same behaviour in their children...a meme is operating." (TCS website at www.tcs.ac)

Dawkins describes memes in this way,

> "The new soup is the soup of human culture. We need a name for the new replicators, a noun which conveys the unit of cultural transmission, or a unit of imitation...Examples of memes are tunes, ideas, catch-phrases, clothes, fashions, ways of making pots or of building arches. Just as gene types propogate themselves in the gene pool by leaping from body to body via sperms or eggs, so memes propogate themselves in the meme pool by leaping from brain to brain via process, which, in the broad sense, can be called imitation." (Dawkins, R., *The Selfish Gene*, chapter 11)

Chapter one

Unwrapping the binding

In Britain today we have a complex and sophisticated system for the delivery of state education. This system is generally viewed as compulsory, although home educators know that in fact it is education and not schooling which is compulsory between the ages of five and sixteen. Despite this, education law consistently talks about 'compulsory school age', and it is commonly assumed that children 'have to' go to school. Furthermore, schooling is free. This does not mean that it costs nothing; on the contrary, it costs a great deal. It means that schooling is free at the point of delivery. Far from this being an enormous benefit, I argue in this book that the effect of 'free', 'compulsory' provision, is actually deeply binding and costly, not only financially, but also in terms of family well-being and skills.

Free, compulsory education has costs. There are financial costs along with a range of other highly detrimental costs to individuals and the society we form. The United Nations Special Rapporteur has more than hinted at this hidden cost in terms of human rights:

"The objective of getting all school-aged children to school and keeping them there until they attain the minimum defined in compulsory education is routinely used in the sector of education, but this objective does not necessarily conform to human rights requirements. In a country where all school-aged children are in school, free of charge, for the full duration of compulsory education, the right to education may be denied or violated. The core human rights standards for education include respect of freedom. The respect of parents' freedom to educate their children according to their vision of what education should be has been part of international human rights standards since their very emergence."
(United Nations Commission on Human Rights, Statement by Special Rapporteur on the Right to Education 8/4/99)

In this chapter I want briefly to outline the main categories of the hidden costs of supposedly 'free' education, including the costs to the very notion of freedom itself.

Really free?

Free education is only free at the point of delivery. Few things are really free and education is no exception. The financial costs to individuals, families and society are high. The cost of educating a nursery or primary aged child in 1998 was £2,080, rising to £2,650 for a secondary aged child (www.statistics.gov.uk). Education is seen as the government's top priority in spending, with pledges of an extra £19 million, that is a budget rise of 5% in each year across the United Kingdom, from 1999-2002. In 1995-1997, spending on education represented 4.9% of gross domestic product (National Statistics p.390) and it was on the basis of this that a spending review pledged the further £19 million. In 1997-1998, education represented the third largest spending category for the government, consuming 13.3% of total government expenditure. (National Statistics p.124)

Despite these figures, there are constant calls for spending on education to be increased. It is commonly assumed that we should be spending as much as possible on education. In the light of this, schemes to target funding into particular areas of need are commonly viewed as economically effective ways of obtaining 'value added' from the children who are required to consume education. In simple terms, children become viewed as units of production with a certain educational base-line 'value' (often a score set through standard attainment tests) to which educational product can be added in order to enhance the educational value of the end-product, in this case a child.

To this end the 'sure-start' project launched in July 1998 to co-ordinate family learning, healthcare and childcare with nursery education has funding of £540 million over three years. (National Statistics p.124). Similarly, the 'National Year of Reading' was launched in September 1998 with an extra £24 million for primary and secondary schools to spend on books. (National Statistics p.129). Money has also been channeled into 'Education Action Zones' with the aim of improving standards in deprived urban and rural regions. (National Statistics p.131).

Of course, children hold the key to future creativity and innovation and should be highly valued members of society. But does it necessarily follow from this that children should be corralled into artificial, costly institutions where they will have the content and method of their learning decreed for them by the state? Are the 93% of school-aged children who attend 'free' state schools really getting value for government and taxpayers' money? Or are they paying the hidden costs of a system which, whilst it claims and undoubtedly intends to be in the children's best interests and for their own good, is actually damaging their intrinsic learning and individual possibilities?

A state system of education funded by taxpayers' money inevitably has certain expectations. It expects that it should get a particular return on its investment. In that sense, children are seen as products that can be measured for value added. One commodity is put in, namely government money; another commodity comes out, namely children who are moulded to fit into a certain society to perform certain functions. There are many voices raised against such objectifications of children as value added products.

John Taylor Gatto sees the whole spectrum of an education which moulds for certain outcomes as a process of 'dumbing down'; John Holt has argued against not just the notion of schooling, but the very notion of education; Ivan Illich has spoken about education being deliberately controlled as a scarce commodity in order to facilitate overall economic control; and thinkers like Aaron Falbel have refined these ideas to critique education as the bastion of corrupt society which we would do better not to raise children to be successful within. From another section of the political spectrum, libertarian thinkers, in particular, those of the *Taking Children Seriously* philosophy, also ask fundamental questions about the morality of objectifying autonomous children as commodities to whom value is added by the input of education. What messages does this send about how we see children as products rather than autonomous moral agents? What are the detrimental effects on intrinsic motivation and creativity?

From a range of critical perspectives the conclusion can be reached that what we are financing when we finance public education is not as straightforward, transparent and obvious as it at first appears. Those who step outside of this system to home-based education, however, find that the transition allows not simply for individualized education to take place in homes, but for the very notion of education *per se* to be critiqued and redefined in a number of ways. Those who do step outside the system have their own financial questions to ask. Parents considering home education are often wary of the cost. The assumption is that a state school will cost them nothing and the costs of providing an education at home must be compared with otherwise paying nothing. Home education certainly has costs, though these vary enormously, depending not only on family circumstances, but also on how education is conceived of or even whether it is conceived as an activity separate from simply living together as a family who want to fulfill a range of preferences. Home educating families are responsible for any educational materials they buy: books, paper, art supplies, computers, software, videos and trips, all have to paid for by the family.

The fact is, however, that many families will make many of these provisions for their children whether or not they home-educate. The marginal cost of extra resources, especially given the availability of libraries, museums, cheap twenty-four hours a day Internet access etc., can be very modest, depending on particular family circumstances. In practice, there are many single parent and low-income home-educating families who do not find the costs prohibitive.

Home education obviously requires that a parent or trusted adult be available for children to ensure that they are safely cared for. This is often a financial concern whether a family has two parents or one. Many people are finding very creative solutions, such as working from home; working an unusual pattern of hours; sharing education and care across families; accessing the support of relatives, especially grandparents; or living in community settings; all possible and practical solutions for some families. Additionally, many families find that it is economically viable to move to one income or two flexible or part time incomes. This is because not only do the obvious costs of childcare, transport to work etc., decrease, but the more relaxed lifestyle frequently means that less luxury items are needed by the family to compensate for living a stressful, busy life. Other advantages, such as free or reduced cost access to many visitor attractions and events and considerably cheaper holidays in quieter term times, also play their part in ensuring that whilst home education is not free, it is affordable.

Nothing is free. It is a considered decision that education, which is free at the point of delivery, has been provided for the last hundred years. Take-up is certainly high with 93% of school-aged children attending state schools (National Statistics p.124). Popularity, however, is not always the best indicator of sound thinking. In an increasingly post modern society in which the factory model of work is less and less common, it is arguable that schools are not a

model of education that either provide for the best future or the best
return for investment. The concept of education as a commodity to
be consumed, a notion on which the school system must rely, is
itself deeply questionable, an issue to which we will return in more
depth in chapter 2.

Questions of welfare
Compulsion always carries its own costs. As mainstream education
becomes more and more prescriptive, it necessitates an increasingly
narrow definition of the typical or normal child who can be defined
as functional within the constraints of the given system.
Compulsory, free education carries with it social costs, including
the rise of medical, psychological and civil liberty intervention into
families under the guise of education.

Thomas Szasz has particularly spoken out against the costs of
merging educational concerns with psychological and welfare
issues. In 'Summary Statement and Manifesto' he contends that:

> *"Mental illness is a metaphor (metaphorical disease). The
> word "disease" denotes a demonstrable biological process
> that affects the bodies of living organisms (plants, animals,
> and humans). The term 'mental illness' refers to the
> undesirable thoughts, feelings, and behaviors of persons.
> Classifying thoughts, feelings, and behaviors as diseases is a
> logical and semantic error, like classifying the whale as a fish.
> As the whale is not a fish, mental illness is not a disease.
> Individuals with brain diseases (bad brains) or kidney
> diseases (bad kidneys) are literally sick. Individuals with
> mental diseases (bad behaviors) like societies with economic
> diseases (bad fiscal policies) are metaphorically sick. The
> classification of (mis)behavior as illness provides an
> ideological justification for state-sponsored social control as
> medical treatment."*

Szasz goes on to highlight the importance of separating state (for
our purposes state educational provision) from psychiatry:

> *"If we recognize that 'mental illness' is a metaphor for
> disapproved thoughts, feelings, and behaviors, we are
> compelled to recognize as well that the primary function of
> Psychiatry is to control thought, mood, and behavior. Hence,
> like Church and State, Psychiatry and the State ought to be
> separated by a 'wall'. At the same time, the State ought not to
> interfere with mental health practices between consenting*

adults. The role of psychiatrists and mental health experts with regard to law, the school system, and other organizations ought to be similar to the role of clergymen in those situations."

The current vogue is for 'joined up government' in which the social, health, education and welfare provisions of the state flow into one another in what seems like a common sense and innocuous avoidance of the duplication of services and resources. Szasz points to the dangers of such thinking. Far from being common sense, this approach allows discrete concepts to slide into one another in muddled thinking. Far from being innocuous, it allows burgeoning systems of control to erode privacy and autonomy. It is true that areas of human activity and need clearly overlap. This does not justify the philosophical confusion of boundaries between welfare and education, particularly when education is defined by a state system that labels a range of individuals dysfunctional because their individual learning styles and preferences do not fit in.

State education has, in many senses, blurred the distinctions and boundaries between educational and welfare provision. This may appear to be good common sense and to serve the holistic interest of the child rather than seeing her piecemeal as a mind to be filled in an educational setting, a body to be treated in a medical or welfare setting etc. Unfortunately, the outcomes may be very much less benevolent. If children are commodities to be invested in and from whom we gain value added as defined by the state (not the individual) then the whole child is objectified as a commodity that must fit and function. In this view, education is not a resource for children to access according to their intrinsic motivation, preferences and best interests by their own lights, but a package to be consumed in order to mould the child. The product, at all stages of production, must be controllable within the framework of the production environment. This control is best achieved when the child is taught not only what to learn, but also how to fit in with particular behavioural, social, medical and other models that best serve the environment. Behavioural traits become redefined as diseases to be treated by psychological intervention, or medication or both.

Home educators, whilst they are able to take a holistic approach to living and learning, do not have to co-operate with these notions of the spread of educational provision into welfare concerns under the cloak of 'holistic' or 'joined up' thinking. There are very good grounds as to why home education is not in itself a welfare issue.

Home education is not a *prima facie* cause for welfare concern! Any attempts to treat it as such should be vigorously resisted. Home education has no national curriculum and follows no single package. For this reason it does not demand such narrow prescriptions of what is 'functional' in order for children to be able to fit into their environment; rather, it allows children's individuality greater latitude. Any assessment of home education provision from outside is not made within the narrow confines of judging a child for conformity to a classroom environment, but only within the much wider and diversely interpreted educational boundaries of suitability according to age, ability and aptitude.

Local Education Authorities have no general welfare remit in regard to home education. They might occasionally come across concerns that should be referred further, but there should be no general policy that home education is grounds for suspicion. Also, a family choosing to provide evidence of their educational provision via means other than a home visit (with or without children present) is not a reasonable cause for suspicion. (For a more detailed discussion of the law relating to home education see Ian Dowty, 'An Outline of the Law and Practice of Home-Based Education' in *Free Range Education*.) Home educators should be free to pursue broad and individual notions of welfare, enjoying diverse lifestyles while giving no cause for concern or risking intervention. Local Education Authorities have very minor duties in relation to home educators. The fact that home educators themselves may have a holistic view of education does not widen LEA powers to inquire beyond age, ability, aptitude and special educational needs. (An issue to which we will return to this in more detail in chapter 3.)

Although the question, 'are the children being checked on?' seems to be a common response to home educating families, we have no national consensus that children must have an institution checking on their welfare at all stages of growing up. We allow preschoolers to go without such checks, so why should the home education community submit to anything more? We know that having an institutional overview of a child is no guarantee of detection of abuse and it would be grossly unrealistic to think that an hour's visit from a stranger with a broad educational remit could achieve this with any regularity or reliability, if at all. Conversely, the pressure on LEA officers not to 'miss something' if they were burdened with a specific welfare monitoring role could conceivably lead to a higher rate of false alarms, with both resulting trauma for the family and serious legal come back on LEAs.

Within the constraints of a visit to assess educational and educational welfare provision, it is unlikely that an officer could reliably infer even serious abuse on most occasions. This could lead to spurious issues becoming grounds for suspicion and traumatic intervention. For example, is a child choosing to wear pyjamas in the day time, or is there a certain amount of dirt around the home, or an untidy house, or closed curtains, an alarm bell, or simply a matter of divergent lifestyle? It would be discriminatory and unacceptable to apply specific 'abuse checks' to only one sector of society, as well as arguably an abuse of public funding, particularly when serious abuse is going undetected elsewhere. Health and safety regulations do not apply to homes. Just as there is a vast range of educational approaches that are legally acceptable, so there are vast ranges of living styles that do not come within the proper scope of welfare concerns, however much they superficially or fundamentally differ from the perceived 'norm' by individual education officers.

It should also be remembered that 'home education' is better seen as 'home-based-education' and, in practice, many venues will be used as educational arenas. This said, it is a fact that some children will fall through any net. Detection of abuse relies on a multi-agency/community approach, including doctors, hospitals, churches, youth organizations, children's charities, playgroups, and so on. Schools are only one part in this and not themselves a foolproof mechanism for detection. Removal from school is not in itself an indicator of abuse unless there are other indicators already in place.

The separation of educational and welfare issues which home educators are able to make in their relations with state and community, are not so easily achieved by children in school. For a growing number of children, and often their whole families, compulsory 'free' schooling comes with a high cost in welfare. Szasz's calls for a separation of state education and health issues, particularly in the arena of mental health, are rarely heard and seldom practiced (as we will explore more fully in chapter 3).

The human costs
A vast range of emotional costs is closely associated with the social costs of compulsory, free schooling. Bullying in schools is now commonplace. The forms bullying takes are as vast as the ingenuity of their attackers. A growing number of children are involved in serious physical assault for which they can find no redress. Despite a plethora of anti-bullying policies, it is often unresolved issues of

chronic and severe bullying, sometimes accompanied by the school's attempts to blame the victim, that lead many parents and children to begin home education. There exists in our society a strong meme that 'bullying is part of life, you just have to learn to deal with it' and those who do not learn to deal with it are as likely, if not more likely, to face 'treatment' than their aggressors. Home education challenges the meme.

Many other children, individuals of all temperaments, find that in such a narrow and conformity-driven culture, they are labelled as dysfunctional. It is easier to blame the individual than to admit that the system cannot cater for the full span of human individuality and learning preferences. Even for those children who are not explicitly labelled, the attack on individuality can be unremitting. The school environment is essentially a coercive one. It aims to deliver a pre-conceived package of education that is motivated by external factors around current government and educational thinking on the best interests of children. I have previously argued that,

> "Coercion damages both our rationality and creativity and ultimately hinders the growth of knowledge. Taking Children Seriously philosophy maintains that coercion is detrimental to rational thinking and therefore damaging to education.... Education and the optimum thought processes needed to learn are not simply or even primarily about being able to memorise and reproduce a received body of knowledge, but are essentially about the ability to create new knowledge and the optimum conditions for creativity and intrinsically motivated learning. We are born with brains that are ideally suited to learning. We are born rational and creative. With the input of information and the unimpeded ability to learn through a continual process of conjecture and refutation, rational thought and creativity will develop and flourish. However, when the process is interrupted by coercion, a line of thought is sabotaged in its tracks and this sabotaging may often be accompanied by painful feelings of being thwarted and left in a state of turmoil. When this sabotaging occurs over and over again, especially in the same area, then in place of rational thinking there will be damaged thinking. Not only is a particular line of learning cut off, but also, in its place, there is likely to be irrationality, poor theories and a decrease in problem solving capacity."

(Fortune-Wood, *Without Boundaries*, p.1)

In contrast to this, autonomous educators and those who follow consensus models of parenting argue that:

> *"True education is about gaining knowledge in those areas in which one wants to gain knowledge. It is about learning those things which are interesting and useful to the individual concerned. We are most likely to achieve that when we proceed rationally. Rational thinking is about genuinely searching for the truth. To do this there has to be the possibility of refutation as well as conjecture and openness to criticism both from oneself and from the theories of others. This does not mean that others, particularly parents, can appeal to their superior authority or experience or to their adherence to bodies of so called authoritative thinking or belief on a particular subject in order to short circuit the process. Rational argument should speak for itself and be willing to give way to new and better theories. Rational interactions play a crucial role in reaching solutions which work for all the parties concerned, in other words in reaching common preferences.*
>
> *"When we choose coercion over and against finding a common preference we not only lose the possibility of new knowledge being created, but also risk impairing our ability to think, learn and solve problems. In situations where there is a problem to be solved, coerced children will abandon the attempt to creatively problem solve, knowing it to be futile since ultimately the solution will be imposed by the adults. Learning does not take place and creativity is trampled. Children need to have successful experiences of finding solutions and having control over their own lives. Coercion replaces this experience with feelings of powerlessness, resentment and frustration, adding painful feelings to areas of thinking and thus adding in another blockage to rational thinking. Whilst coercion helps to convince children that life is difficult, that getting what one wants is next to impossible and that doing things one hates is inevitable, non-coercion creates flexible thinkers who see that they can control their lives and have lives which they want to live."*
>
> (Fortune-Wood, *Without Boundaries*, pp.22-23)

Intrinsic learning and coercion are inimical. Children who find that their intrinsic motivation is more than slightly out of step with the externally motivated learning package, or who show resistance to the demands of the structure, quickly find themselves bearing a label that is seen to justify a range of interventions of increasing coercion and potential damage. The brunt of the human cost of the bullying and labelling, now endemic in schools, is being born by younger and younger children.

Despite the warnings of Commons Select Committee on Education concerning the detrimental effects of admitting younger children to formal school-based education, the push for 'education, education, education', even for the youngest children, shows little sign of abating. In 1998 62% of all three and four year-olds were in school, compared to 45% in 1982. (www.statistics.gov.uk) Currently, 57% of four-year-olds are in full time infant classes, fully engaged in the requirements of the National Curriculum.

The coercion experienced in the school system, with its culture of bullies and labels, derives its power entirely from parental complicity. Tragically, many parents remain ignorant of this. School is *not* compulsory. The duty of education legally rests not with the state, but with parents. The notion wrongly persists that we have no alternative to sending our children into an environment over which we have little control, to be taught things they do not want to know, to be prey to violence (only to be accused of having 'victim mentalities') and to be subject to a range of psychological or medical intervention if they do not conform. The most damaging coercion is to have parents who are patently not on the child's side, even when this involves good and loving parents who are simply ignorant. The human cost of 'free' education can be halted with a simple letter of deregistration or by choosing never to delegate educational responsibility to schools.

The myth of expertise
Compulsory, free education removes learning not only from the learner's control, but also from the parents' sphere of influence. Both parents and children are de-skilled by a system that perpetuates the myth that expert teachers are central to real learning. The concept of skilled families is replaced by the judgment of families who are either conforming and consequently 'good', or non-conforming and consequently 'bad' or dysfunctional. The notion of autonomous, rational children is replaced with the idea of dependent sub-humans, not fit to be treated as moral agents in their own right, with little or no insight into their own learning needs and goals.

There is undoubtedly a role for expertise in modern life. We cannot all know everything. Skill and knowledge specialisations and the interdependence that comes from them are a foundation for human progress and prosperity. This does not, however, justify the bogus professionalisation of learning *per se*. Learning and whatever teaching, perhaps better characterized as facilitating and helping, that goes with it, is a human activity that can never be contained within a state institution. Learning is an activity of life and introducing compulsion and extrinsic motivation into this activity not only impedes the intrinsic growth of knowledge, but is unlikely to have precisely the outcomes which educators intend, since the 'products' are not passive, but complex autonomous human people.

It might well be the case that schooling is set up with the 'best interests' of children in mind, but the very act of defining these best interests for another human being, and then compounding this basic error by coercing children into schools, negates the intention, however laudable. It is a big jump from saying that experts serve a useful purpose and ought to be listened to with very serious consideration when they speak within their given field, to asserting that children cannot learn without teachers. The logic is simply not apparent; nor is this the experience of thousands of home-educated children and their parents. One parent commented:

> *"I feel that this (i.e. the need for expert teachers) is an erroneous idea that is often used as an argument against home education, especially by parents who DON'T home educate but want to justify why they don't. Even teachers in secondary schools do not have that much expertise. It is quite possible to keep up with any given area of study by using textbooks and the Internet. If a parent felt really out of depth in an area they can always get a tutor to do some extra work with the home-educated children."*

Most parents, however unconfident they might feel, take it for granted that (barring insurmountable disabilities) their child will learn to walk, to talk, to perform a burgeoning number of complex functions and display a huge array of learning before the idea of schooling ever surfaces. Yet, extraordinarily, parents fear that these same children will stop learning and fall into ignorant savagery if they are not forced to go to school at increasingly young ages and there learn what the so-called experts dictate. The meme that school and teachers are the essential properties of learning is as false as it is widespread. We all know that learning takes place on a much grander and more unpredictable scale than schools can ever cater to; yet we persist with the cult of expert teachers. Why?

The reasons are legion, but one key issue is that schools, apart from any learning agenda that they ostensibly have, have become the bastions of free childcare; much to the relief and convenience of many parents. Schools absolve parents from the responsibility of being the primary helpers in the lives of their children. The whole edifice of conventional parenting, which sees children as problems to be solved, bolsters the idea that school is a good solution; children are not only occupied, out of sight, but are 'getting an education' and a free one at that, into the bargain.

Along with this convenience and lessening of responsibility, comes a cost, which itself becomes another reason for continuing to believe the myth. Parents and children alike are deskilled and made dependent by the myth that learning requires teachers. Parents come to believe that they could not possibly compete with the learning opportunities available within schools, often without ever questioning whether they are even remotely relevant to their children. Children come to believe that without coercion they would be lazy, unmotivated and lapse into stupidity.

Home education explodes these myths. Parents and children are ideally placed to develop their own spheres of expertise and to access the expertise of the communities, geographical or virtual, in which they live. Dispensing with schoolteachers does not mean dispensing with experts. Many home-educated children find creative ways to locate just the kind of expert help that their intrinsic motivations require. It might involve hiring a music tutor; it might involve posting a question on an academic board on an Internet newsgroup; it might entail phoning a local university professor or going to an archeological dig or a veterinary surgery or an artist's studio. The methods are as disparate as the human imagination allows. The common thread is that the learner is centre stage, accessing the information and resources required for his own pursuits with the aid of parents who will give all the help they can. Home education is not anti-expertise; it is anti-external-agenda in education. At is best, it uses expertise much more richly than schools can ever hope to, and always by the child's own lights.

In this respect, home education has three characteristics. It is inevitably more creative and flexible. It is at the cutting edge of educational thinking, especially as society becomes increasingly postmodern, event-driven and flexible. Schools serve an outdated notion of society based on factories, large offices and inflexible chains of command. As society moves away from that model at an increasing pace, schools are ill-placed to adapt; the structural and institutional model which is so fundamental to their identity simply militates against the message of flexibility, creative thinking and autonomy that home education is perfectly placed to engender.

A second characteristic of home-based education is that it tends to give rise to learning which is more diverse than the learning allowed for within any curriculum.   Across a spectrum of home-educated children, some individual children may exhibit passions and knowledge that are more specialised, deeper, and perhaps more idiosyncratic than their school-going peers.   School curricula sell the myth of education that needs to be 'broad and balanced'. Behind this rhetoric is the fact that in trying to cater for everyone, schools opt for small amounts of shallow, disjointed knowledge, much of which will be irrelevant and forgotten by most of the learners at any one time. Home education is much more efficient. If children seem to be following their passions to the exclusion of other areas, we would do well to remember that most of life's real experts found ways of doing just the same, often in spite of the school system.

Home education tends to be less predictable than school education. It is arguable that the predictability of school education is itself a charade, and that the concepts of value-added and outcomes applied to children are not ultimately effective even within the system they serve.   Home educators who respect the autonomy of children as learners are not likely to be able to decide where it is all leading. It demands a certain amount of serendipity, much vigilance for clues of what learning and resources might be helpful, and a great deal of trust and optimism.   These things are not only possible, but are ultimately the only moral way assist our children in getting the education they want.

Liberating education
There are two distinct kinds of free education. The state provision of education is free at the point of delivery, but its compulsory and coercive nature hides a whole range of far-reaching costs. In the next four chapters, I will examine the costs outlined above in more detail. I will argue that education that is actually 'free' is education that promotes the most diverse model of human liberty. Home education certainly demands an input of resources, whether in time, money or raw commitment to our own children. If we want our children to be conforming, homogenous products then it is not the path to take. If we value autonomy and true freedom in education, we have an established, growing and flourishing alternative in the thousands of home educating families who are already re-defining what education means.

Home education is not merely a negative expedient in the face of a failing system, but a positive range of educational choices. As there is no national curriculum for home education, both the theory and practice of home education varies widely across the families who enjoy it. Despite this vast breadth of philosophies encompassed by home education, it is united in a range of positive features.

The learning environment can be precisely tailored to individual learning styles and preferences. One child might prefer to work in a stimulating environment, full of sound and colour, while another chooses a calm, quiet environment. The friendly learning environment focuses on strengths, building self-confidence and self-esteem. Criticism comes only as something constructive and welcome. The child (together with his or her family) defines and creates the environment rather than the environment defining (and labelling) the child.

Families practicing home-based education are free to pursue event-driven lifestyles rather than clock-driven lifestyles, allowing maximum flexibility and access to an increasingly event-driven society. Government-controlled curriculum is replaced with the positive idea of learning dictated by the intrinsic motivation of the child and/or the educational philosophy of the family. Home education, even in its more structured forms, helps children develop research skills as they increasingly learn to manage their own learning. This equips them to be real researchers and producers of knowledge, not just consumers of pre-defined educational packages. Home education naturally promotes a sense of being in control and responsible, part of a wider vision of developing and supporting moral and humane family and societal institutions.

Children remain a full part of local communities with the ability fully to access community facilities, such as libraries, shops, museums, exhibitions, theatres, transport, art centres and so on. In the familiar and small scale environment of the home, supplemented by access to the community and its facilities, home-educated children are able to employ what Roland Meighan has called 'purposive conversation' as their primary learning tool, to great effect. In other words, there is a great deal of space within family life without the pressure of school to facilitate far-ranging educational opportunities and growth of knowledge on the basis of what might begin as incidental questions or conversational asides.

Home education allows education that, whilst it may not be 'free' in financial terms, can be uniquely 'freeing' in individual and human terms. It is an education that offers a children much more than one model into which they must fit, putting the individual children at centre stage in their own production of knowledge.   Home education has the potential to be 'really free', not because it costs nothing (a state which can, in any case, lead to something being unvalued) but by developing alternative models of educational thought and practice which affects every aspect of lifestyle. I will return to this theme in depth in chapter six to contend that home education is free, i.e. liberating, educating because it enables children and parents together to maximise the philosophical control of what we mean by education; retain the control of the content of education; nurture an ethos in which respect for children's autonomy and civil liberty is paramount; promote divergence in educational theory and practice; advance a pro-active culture of finding and accessing and foster event-driven living.

All human activity entails choices, yet the pervasiveness of the belief that schooling is compulsory is so dominant that many children are sent to school at five or four or even three without any conscious choice having been made. This façade of inevitability masks the truth that children do not have to go to school. Many do so, not out of choice, but because of parental ignorance or because parents willfully pretend that school is compulsory for their own convenience. There is nothing bad in itself about convenience. We are used to the idea that items that make life more convenient are often also those that are expensive. If we want to eat convenience foods we pay to do so and it is our own business.

It is quite another matter, however, when we pay for some convenience, in this case the convenience of not having to think about childcare and education, with someone else's liberty. Home education presents us with another way of thinking, not only about 'education, education, education', but about 'life, life, life', so that the costs of education are not emotionally and rationally exorbitant. And especially, so that they are not paid at children's expense.

Chapter two

Nothing is free

The myth of 'free' education masks the true **financial** costs to individuals, families and society. In this chapter, I will contend that the dominance and ubiquitous nature of this provision has wrongly focused the responsibility and accountability for education in state machinery. I will go on to argue that since financial control and philosophical control inevitably go hand in hand, parents must take back the former if they value the latter.

State education is costly. Not only do most people think that the cost is worthwhile, but the problems of education are generally characterised as arising from under-investment, rather than the reverse. No amount of funding can compete with tailor-made education, which children initiate and control. The state has no reason to be in the business of providing such an education. Rather, it provides a package which best meets a specific agenda of conformity and product requirement. Since it is funded by taxpayers' money, it is inevitable that this package should be quantifiable, with predictable and measurable outcomes. The more money that is invested, the more the quality of the product must bear scrutiny, at least in theory. This is, after all, public money to be properly accounted for. Investment buys control. Despite the rhetoric of home-school contracts, co-operation and consultation, the balance of control must always reside firmly with the funders.

Delegating our responsibility for our children's education to schools is a serious undertaking. Parents and children cannot pick and choose the parts of the system that suit their individual requirements. School is not designed as a resource to be accessed by individuals at will, but as the delivery mechanism in forming a particular society. (A few children who attend without compulsion and whom have parents dedicated to working with them creatively may be able to treat school differently, but these tend to be the exception.) The resources currently being channeled towards exclusions and truancy evidence the monolithic and inflexible intent of the school system. Police have new powers under the Crime and

Disorder Act, and the government is spending £500 million on a three-year package to reduce exclusion and truancy figures, including a reduction of one-third in truancy rates by the year 2002. If parents do not exercise their right to not delegate children's education to schools, then public money is committed whether or not those children go to school. Money paid for children who vote with their feet and opt out of the provision without the system's consent are seen as wasting public funds. There is a perceived failure of accountability. The government react to this not by questioning why the provision is failing these children, but by committing extra money to ensure that 90% of children registered are actually consuming the resources that have been paid for on their behalf, even if this consumption amounts to no more than physical attendance.

Not everyone shares the educational system's view of what constitutes success, citizenship, or education. Increasingly, there are serious criticisms concerning the delegation of parental responsibility to educate children, along with fundamental questions about children as products, about who holds philosophical control of education, and even about what education is. The voices raised against the educational system's objectification of children are diverse; representing different understandings of what 'free' education might look like.

In place of education and materialism
John Taylor Gatto calls the whole spectrum of an education which moulds for certain outcomes, a process of 'dumbing down'. He objects that 'free', mass schooling has the effect not of educating children, but of teaching a hidden curriculum of dependency.

> *"None of this is inevitable. None of it is impossible to overthrow. We do have choices in how we bring up young people; there is no one right way."*
>
> (Gatto, *Dumbing Us Down*, chapter 3)

Gatto detects a strong link between mass schooling and what he sees as the ills of society, ills that he also puts down to the rise of mass entertainment through television and large-scale consumerism. He goes on to call for education to look backwards to a time before mass schooling, when simpler lifestyles and closer families were the orders of the day. For Gatto, globalisation and modern economic interests collude to require a dumbed down population. The increasing cost of state education is the cost of maintaining this complacent, unthinking mass. Education becomes a self-perpetuating and self-serving machine, which puts the needs of business before the needs of people.

> *"Global economics does not speak to the public need for meaningful work, affordable housing, fulfilling education, adequate medical care, a clean environment, honest and accountable government, social and cultural renewal, or simple justice. All global ambitions are based on a definition of productivity and the good life so alienated from common human reality I am convinced it is wrong and that most people would agree with me if they could perceive an alternative. We might be able to see that if we regained a hold on a philosophy that locates meaning where meaning is genuinely to be found - in families, in friends, in the passage of seasons, in nature, in simple ceremonies and rituals, in curiosity, generosity, compassion, and service to others, in a decent independence and privacy, in all the free and inexpensive things out of which real families, real friends, and real communities are built- then we would be so self-sufficient we would not even need for the material "sufficiency" which our global "experts" are so insistent we be concerned about."*

(Gatto, *Dumbing Us Down*, chapter 3)

The economic agenda of education is neither what it is proclaimed to be, nor neutral.

> *"Look again at the seven lessons of schoolteaching - confusion, class position, indifference, emotional and intellectual dependency, conditional self-esteem, surveillance - all of these lessons are prime training for permanent underclasses... the growth of ... profit from schooling ... has enlarged this institution's original grasp to the point that it now seizes the sons and daughters of the middle classes as well."*

(Gatto, *Dumbing Us Down*, chapter 3)

Gatto sees a conspiracy in which 'free' education is deliberately expensive, since a whole raft of businesses; commercial interests and employment rely on it:

> *"... The method is deeply and profoundly anti-educational. No tinkering will fix it. In one of the great ironies of human affairs, the massive rethinking the schools require would cost so much less than we are spending now that powerful interests cannot afford to let it happen. You must understand that first and foremost the business I am in is a **jobs project** and an*

agency for letting contracts. We cannot afford to save money
by reducing the scope of our operation or by diversifying the
product we offer, even to help children grow up right. That is
the iron law of institutional schooling - it is a business, not
subject to the rational scalpel of competition.

"Some form of free-market system in public schooling is the
likeliest place to look for answers, a free market where family
schools and small entrepreneurial schools and religious
schools and craft schools and farm schools exist in profusion
to compete with government education. I'm trying to describe
to a free market in schooling exactly like the one the country
had until the Civil War, **one in which students volunteer for**
the kind of education that suits them, *even if that means self-*
education;..."

(Gatto, *Dumbing Us Down,* chapter 3)

While Gatto might espouse a conspiracy theory that goes beyond
what many would support, it is an interesting notion that state
education is enormously expensive in comparison to self-motivated,
self-directed education. Once we accept that education is the
preserve of experts (a theme to which we will return in chapter 5)
the cost necessarily escalates and the economics of vested interest
certainly begin to play a major role in educational provision.

Gatto's utopia of education is not one that everyone would want to
buy into. The simple, self-sufficient lifestyle lived for the good of
the community, in which the 'natural' predominates and modern
influences like television and mass entertainment are banished, is
not the utopian vision of those who want to build and nurture
education around their children's intrinsic motivations. Although
Gatto clearly offers some illuminating insights I would be anxious
that Gatto's vision could, in itself, become educationally restrictive.

"...Television does...have the advantage of being an
incredibly diverse source of easily accessed information.
Moreover, it is a deeply effective medium for communicating
culture and a fascinating source of information on how the
world and people operate. Fears about a child watching
'inappropriate material' (usually anything which is deemed to
have a sexual or violent content) are simply based on asking
the wrong question. How can we get from assuming that
children are born innately rational, trustworthy and good, to
believing that if given a TV they will instantly become
irrational, self-destructive and bad? Children in non-coercive
homes will choose to watch the things which further the

*learning that only they can know is going on in their own
minds. They will choose content which has meaning to them,
which helps them explore the questions they are ready to
explore, which can be safely and fruitfully followed up in
conversations with parents and other trusted adults.
'Appropriate' viewing is whatever fits into this category.*

*"...Television does not exert negative influences, it is a
neutral object, but imposing coercive restrictions around its
use causes irrationality. Denying someone access to the
information, ideas and entertainment that television provides,
cuts off a whole arena of intrinsically motivated learning. It
can never be for the child's own good. For a parent to take
away a child's autonomy and behave as though the child is
too irrational or stupid or bad to make her own decisions,
based on hearing all the theories, can only interfere with the
child's growth of knowledge."*

(Fortune-Wood, *Doing It Their Way*, pp.80-82)

This criticism aside, Gatto does rightly point to a scale of cost for
mass 'free' schooling that may not ultimately be justified as being
in anyone's best interests. Whether home educating families take
Gatto's stance and eschew modern high-tech, high entertainment
lifestyles in favour of the back-to-basics, self-supporting model, or
take the opposite route of availing themselves of every modern
media, the cost will tend to be cheaper.

Moreover, mass education, while proliferating the cult of experts
and taking up increasingly larger percentages of the national budget,
is also touted as a scarce commodity; children are urged to compete
to avail themselves of this resource while they can. In response to
this, Ivan Illich argues that the concept of education as a scarce
commodity is a deliberate tactic of overall economic control.
Discussing this in *Growing Without Schooling*, Aaron Falbel quotes
Illich:

*"Economics always implies the assumption of scarcity. What
is not scarce cannot be subjected to economic control. This is
as true of goods and services as it is of work. The assumption
of scarcity has penetrated all modern institutions. Education
is built on the knowledge that desirable knowledge is
scarce.... The identification of that which is desirable with
that which is scarce has deeply shaped our thinking, our
feeling, our perception of reality itself."*

(Falbel, quoting Illich, *Growing Without Education*,
GWS issue 30, p.29)

The existence of home educating families, many living and educating on very limited budgets, puts the lie to this scarcity. Not only is intrinsically motivated education neither necessarily expensive nor scarce, but also the very notion of what we mean by education *per se* is challenged. Falbel goes on to quote a CBC radio interview with Illich in which Illich makes the point that it is only when knowledge is packaged and given a value tag that education comes to mean:

> "...*learning under the assumption that the means for this purpose are scarce. If I had only one desire, it would be to get across to the people who study education...that they should not study what happens in education, but how the very idea of this nonsense could have come into existence.*"
> (Falbel, quoting Illich, *Growing Without Education,*
> GWS issue 30, p.29)

A 'free' mass schooling system, funded by the state, can never afford to ask these questions. It is fundamental to the existence of such a system that something precious and hard to obtain anywhere else is being offered. It is essential for such a system to perpetrate the theory that the coercion and loss of civil liberties involved, together with the psychological and emotional pressures to ensure that individual children function smoothly within the environment are small prices to pay for such a rare product. Not everyone is convinced. Taking up Illich's desire to deconstruct the very idea of education, Holt has argued against not just the notion of schooling, but also the very notion of education. In *Instead of Education,*

> "*Education...now seems to me perhaps the most authoritarian and dangerous of all the social inventions of mankind. It is the deepest foundation of the modern slave state, in which most people feel themselves to be nothing but producers, consumers, spectators and 'fans', driven more and more, in all parts of their lives, by greed, envy and fear. My concern is not to improve 'education' but to do away with it, to end the ugly and antihuman business of people shaping and help people to shape themselves.*"
> (John Holt, *Instead of Education,* quoted in Falbel,
> *Growing Without Education,* GWS issue 30, p.29)

Thinkers like Falbel have refined these ideas in order to criticise education as the bastion of a corrupt society. He and others raise the question of whether we would do better not to raise children to be successful within such systems.

"Education props up and bolsters the absurdities of the modern world. Education as people shaping, whether it happens at school or at home, is geared towards making people fit in... Now, we all want our children to be successful don't we? Not necessarily. If we agree with Holt and Illich that society is in as bad a shape as they say it is, then becoming a success in such a society may be the worst thing we could wish for our children. In an overly materialistic, tremendously voracious, wasteful, exploitative, consumptive, technophilic, militaristic, competitive society being a successful, functioning member would only compound the problem."

(Aaron Falbel, *Growing Without Education*,
GWS issue 30, pp.29-30)

Falbel recognizes that such a critique of education and of the economic base of 'free' mass schooling comes from a very specific political outlook that is not shared across the breadth of home educators. He goes on,

"Most of us grew up viewing progress and development as 'good things,' but decades of pollution, environmental degradation, social polarization, resource depletion and frustrated expectations, have convinced some of us otherwise....Education as preparation-for-life teaches that the good life necessarily involves a scramble for scarce resources."

Falbel makes some laudable points and raises some vital questions, but it is, as he acknowledges himself, a critique that rests on some very specific assumptions, which themselves bear scrutiny. There is the suspicion, even though Falbel does not press his arguments to their logical conclusion, that progress and the technologies which accompany it, perhaps particularly the availability of mass entertainment and information through television and other modern media, are corrupting and dehumanizing. It would not take an immense leap in thinking to use Falbel's critiques as a platform for the assumption that the enjoyment of these mass means of communication and entertainment is itself proof that children are empty buckets into whom unhealthy influences can be poured against their will, for the benefit of global economic interests. We need to guard against moving from a critique of society and culture to any justification of a simplistic view of children's ability to sift theories and culture for themselves. After all, many of today's pioneers themselves grew up on a diet of so-called 'junk' and adeptly not only survived the influences, but used them to work out new knowledge for themselves. We need to be wary of attempting to second guess the developmental process of minds that we cannot see into.

Alongside the ideas that arise from the thinking of writers like Falbel and Gatto is the concept that, rescued from the notion of education as it is packaged in schools, society would move back to some kind of 'golden age' in which community comes before individuals and pursuits are 'natural'. It is a critique that has the potential to become every bit as coercive as any state schooling system. As I commented in *Doing It Their Way* when discussing 'natural' approaches to autonomous learning,

> *"Being allowed to develop naturally can sound so like being free to develop autonomously, but the two are not the same. Natural development is actually strictly controlled according to a preordained agenda of what it means to be 'natural', whereas autonomy has no agenda. 'Rightness' and 'naturalness' are not epithets that can ultimately hide the coercive nature of any education... Projecting any 'mystical', 'unspoilt' qualities onto children is ultimately demeaning. It traps children in an adult, romanticised fantasy of what it means to be a child. This is not autonomy.*

> *"...On the face of it this sounds like autonomy, but it is not, simply because it comes with an agenda and with a fixed product in mind a...child who fulfils a list of product specifications based on an idealised understanding of what is natural to human nature.*

> *"...Unfortunately, what is defined as 'natural' can too easily become a replacement for curricula. It might, for example, be that the child is free to develop, but it is expected that the natural, magical child will choose sanctioned foods, play with wooden toys, avoid arcade-style computer games, television and gun play. Whilst these areas are not ones which would conventionally be considered to be central to autonomous education, real autonomy does demand that intrinsic motivation is essential for all learning. Limiting intrinsic motivation by any means, however subtly communicated, limits and severely hinders or damages thought processes."*
> (Fortune-Wood, *Doing It Their Way*, pp.31-33)

Despite these dangers, Gatto, Holt and Illich offer important insights into the whole thesis that education is a costly and scarce commodity, which only the state (or the very rich) can afford and which must be delivered by experts. Education as we know it is expensive because it is externally motivated. It is financially costly to deliver highly generalised pre-ordained packages to a captive audience for eleven years of their childhood. By contrast, whilst some home educators might **choose** to make significant financial outlay for their children's learning opportunities, many find that they can achieve intrinsically motivated goals on a range of budgets down to the very small, often employing creativity as their major resource. Home educators do not have to take an anti-materialistic, anti-technology stance in their pursuit of new definitions of education. We can embrace technology and take children seriously as the arbiters of their own preferences in learning and still contend that the current budget required to provide 'free' mass state schooling is not an inevitable price to pay for an educated society. Falbel recognises this to some extent when he writes,

"Growing Without Education *questions whether any of us - even parents - have the right to treat young people like lumps of clay which they can shape however they wish, or mould according to 'society's needs'. Instead* GWE *asks us to trust children... It assumes that young people do not need to undergo educational treatment if they are to make sense of the world..."*
(Aaron Falbel, *Growing Without Education,* GWS issue 30, p.30)

This is a crucial point. Free state schooling has costs, enormous financial costs. It can also have high personal costs, not because children are empty buckets just waiting to be filled with the latest progressive effluent of modern society, but because parents, the very people who children most rely upon to protect and help them, instead coerce them into monolithic institutions where their intrinsic motivation to learn is supplanted by someone else's agenda. The parental collusion with the myth that schooling is compulsory is enormously damaging to real education. There is nothing to be gained by replacing this coercion with home education that similarly wants to mould and produce children as particular, but different products, even in the name of producing something 'natural' or 'alternative'. The benefits of home education are most fully appreciated when the family reclaims what is meant by the 'best interest of the child' and define for themselves what is 'education' and 'not education', especially when the autonomous child, supported by parental helpers, can live and learn without having to dissect life for what is educational content and what is not.

The morality of education

Those who question the very nature of education do not all do so from the stance of wanting to deconstruct modern economics and society. Replying to Falbel's article in *Growing Without Schooling*, Manoj Padki writes,

> *"I prefer the term self-directed learning. ... this term locates the seat of the process where it truly belongs - with the learner...*
>
> *"The Web has revolutionized access to all kinds of information. Today, practically everything that has ever been thought up by any human being...is accessible at close to zero cost! This revolution is democratizing access to knowledge...it is the next big step in the evolution of humankind itself."*
>
> (Manoj Padki, *More on Growing Without Education*,
> GWS issue 132, p.14)

Padki goes on to dispute that modern progress is either dehumanizing or evil:

> *"The facts I see on the ground lead me to a more optimistic assessment....positive changes have occurred the most in free-market oriented liberal democracies...it is this culture that has empowered self-directed learners the most.*
>
> *"...I see a new society that is a paradise for self-directed learners like me. The recent technological revolution has resulted in a world that is being literally personalized to fit you. The logical end-point of this process is a world where the individual is the arbiter of everything, and you are empowered to become all you can be."*
>
> (Manoj Padki, *More on Growing Without Education*,
> GWS issue 132, p.14)

Of course, Padki's vision of progress has a specific application within largely western and democratic societies. There is an acknowledgement that liberal democracy and the absence of intellectual tyranny are critical factors for self-directed learning. The *Taking Children Seriously* philosophy takes a similarly libertarian stance, examining the morality of objectifying autonomous children as commodities to whom value is added by the input of education. Like Padki, it does so not from the standpoint of advocating a pre-industrial, pre-market world view, but on the basis that it is immoral for parents to infringe upon the autonomy of their children, even on the grounds of 'love' or 'best interests'. As I argue in *Without Boundaries*:

"TCS philosophy maintains that coercion is detrimental to rational thinking and therefore damaging to education... Education and the optimum thought processes needed to learn are not simply or even primarily about being able to memorise and reproduce a received body of knowledge, but are essentially about the ability to create new knowledge and the optimum conditions for creativity and intrinsically motivated learning"

These optimum conditions are found when children can pursue their intrinsic motivation, similar to Padki's notion of empowering individuals who are arbiters of their own lives and learning.

"For knowledge to grow, self-interest functions as both an educational principle and a proper foundation for parenting. ...The conventional assumption is that children are born uncivilised, even wicked, and that their wants will inevitably be bad for themselves and for others, at least for a significant amount of the time, unless they are reigned in. Consent-based parenting, on the other hand, assumes that being 'self-centred' and doing the moral thing co-exist.

"Self-interest is, in fact, the only way to guarantee that those activities engaged in and decisions made are the right ones for any particular individual's learning, growth and well being...This is because the parents are likely to be working on a preconceived agenda of what is best for children in general or from their own perceptions of the child...

"Parents are often concerned that if they concede that their children should act out of self-interest, they will be encouraging their children to become monsters who act immorally and with no regard for other people. ... Doing the most optimal thing for one's own self-interest includes doing the right thing. Where it appears to someone that this is not the case, then it is reason and not coercion that is our best tool in convincing the protagonist otherwise."

(Jan Fortune-Wood, *Without Boundaries*, pp. 30-32.)

Falbel remains unconvinced:

"Sadly, I fear that Manoj is correct when he observes that 'the logical end-point of this process (the technological revolution) is a world where the individual is the arbiter of everything, and you are empowered to become all you can be.'...I am saddened because I hear in this news not only a dangerous hubris but also the death knell of community and the

furtherance of this dog-eat-dog, sink-or-swim, I've-got-mine world we're so intent on creating."

The proponents of TCS would, I think rightly, reply that individual autonomy and empowerment is simply not the opposite of moral living or a wealth of benefits for others. We can afford to be more optimistic, to trust the children who Falbel has previously urged should be trusted. In the final analysis, an anti-materialistic critique of education runs the risk of simply replacing one form of coercion with another. 'Free' education, which costs the taxpayer dearly and which costs children their liberty, could simply be replaced by alternative communitarian notions of what the really good alternative child product would look like. We need to be more radical in our thinking, to move beyond any arguments about what kind of product, to asserting that children are not products at all, but autonomous humans whose intrinsic motivation, when supported, nurtured and facilitated, can be trusted to be in their own best interests without destroying the prospects of others. We need to be wary of moving from the argument that free, compulsory schooling is detrimental to intrinsic motivation, to assuming that we can decide ahead of events what intrinsic motivation is going to look like on a societal or individual scale. To do so would be pre-emptive and presumptuous.

Whilst not everyone would share his economic perspective, writers like Padki and the thinkers of the TCS movement, like Sarah Lawrence, take a genuinely optimistic view of human nature and progress to support the idea that children are not products and that the intrinsic motivation of learners of any age can be trusted to serve the individual optimally and, in so doing, have benefits to society that could never be designed in or predicted. Discussing the idea that we cannot educate for greatness, David Deutsch, taking the example of Winston Churchill, notes that 'greatness' is always a by-product.

"The principal product is satisfaction and fulfillment for the person concerned - and that may be achieved with or without changing the world - though it is almost always good for the world in some way.

"Thus the nine-year-old Winston Churchill, playing with his toy soldiers and generating the knowledge that would later save civilization, was principally striving to give meaning to his own, inner world, to create happiness and fulfillment for himself. And if, in the end, he seems to have succeeded rather

*less well at the principal task than at the side effect, note that in almost all the areas relevant to the principal task, he had no autonomy, but was trapped in a condition of what he later called 'vile servitude'. He achieved greatness in a narrow, initially quite private, area of his own making, of which his educators had no inkling and in which they had no power to interfere. Had they interfered in it, and steered it in (say) a direction that **they** thought fitting for a future Prime Minister, what chance is there that they would not have ruined everything?"*

(David Deutsch, *Education For Greatness,* TCS Journal 27)

Perhaps those most commonly associated with defending both the freedom for personal development and economic freedom are libertarians, but even here there is surprisingly little written on liberty when the subjects are children. The movement does contain some acknowledgement that home education is likely to engender creativity and freedom, but there still exists remarkably little criticism of the notion of education as a package to produce a product, as the following quote from a libertarian web site demonstrates,

"Side by side with public education's lackluster results, the richness of home schooling's achievement - the wealth of challenging subjects its pupils learn, the civility it inculcates, the strong characters it seems to form, and the nurturing family life it reinforces - embodies a practical ideal of childhood and education that can serve as a useful benchmark of what is possible in turn-of-the-millennium America.

"Though existing data are incomplete, everything we know about home-schooled kids says that they are flourishing academically in every way. This year, home-schooled kids swept the top three places on the National Spelling Bee, and Stanford accepted 27 percent of its home-schooled applicants, nearly twice its average acceptance rate. Small wonder that the public school establishment wants to regulate home schooling out of existence. It represents a silent, but eloquent, reproach to the professionals."

(www.free-market.net/directorybytopic/homeschooling)

There is certainly recognition that the high cost of free state schooling is unwarranted,

> *"with a minimum of government interference (home education) has produced literate students at a fraction of the cost of any government program."*
>
> (Isabel Lyman, Cato Insititute,
> www.free-market.net/directorybytopic/homeschooling)

Similarly, there is some recognition that the school model as a monolithic institution is no more appropriate to post-modern society than it is to alternative, back-to-nature utopias,

> *"In a world that is moving lightning fast, the nineteenth century one-size-fits-all model sits like syrup in sand, slowing everything down and wasting our most precious resource: the potential of the human mind."*
>
> (www.libertarian.org/policy2.html)

In general, however, libertarian thought needs to go much further in questioning the product mentality as an appropriate one to apply to our children. Some libertarians are beginning to go further. Stefan Blankertz, for example, in his article, *The Manufacture of Subjection: A Critique of Compulsory State Education* (Rotterdam 1991) argues that,

> *"State interference in education is one of the long-run instruments to manufacture subjects.*
>
> *"Criticizing State interference in education is more challenging than most other libertarian positions. The belief in the need for State interference in education is so deeply rooted in modernity that even most classical liberals, including the most radical of them, rarely doubted the wisdom of such interference."*
>
> (Blankertz, 'The Manufacture of Subjection: A Critique of Compulsory State Education')

Blankertz goes on to argue, following Paul Goodman, that,

> *"It is not the content communicated by State regulated education which matters, Paul Goodman argued, but the fact of coercion itself destroys self-reliance. When people are deprived of the control over their lives and subsequently feeling powerless, they are eager to identify with the ruling force in order to regain some feeling of power. This psychological mechanism was called by Paul Goodman "the psychology of being powerless." That is, the State overwhelms*

us by violence and in return we give the State the "sanction of the victims," as Ayn Rand put it.

"… I am speaking of the State in general whether it be a democracy or a dictatorship or any other conceivable variety of government."
(Blankertz, 'The Manufacture of Subjection: A Critique of Compulsory State Education')

The Taking Children Seriously philosophy might be more likely to interject that the coercion that Blankertz detects, at least in countries where home education is legal, originates in the family and in parents who collude with the falsehood that schooling is compulsory and that children must go to school. Blankertz continues:

"Every action of the State has an "educational" aspect insofar as it educated people into a psychology of subjugation. But for practical reasons I concentrate on the two main educational institutions set up by the State, the family and the schools, which affect all citizens.

"...the State interferes in the family structure, thereby changing its social significance. The State grants the parents control over the children up to an artificially set age. This deeply affects family relationships. As a result the family is not a freely formed group living together by internally agreed upon rules as long as they want to, for at least some members of the family are forced to stay by an outside power.

"...The family is changed from a social arrangement structured by mutual free interactions to a political hierarchy.

The early lesson the child learns from the politicised family is that it does not own itself but is owned by someone else."
(Blankertz, *The Manufacture of Subjection: A Critique of Compulsory State Education*)

This control may be the intent of much family legislation, but advocates of *Taking Children Seriously* have found it possible to make significant paradigm shifts within their families, such that the political hierarchy and the psychology of subjugation do not prevail and are not inevitable. TCS families have found it possible to live without significant interference. In an ideal world the removal of the threat of such interference would make TCS an easier parenting and educational option, but we do not have to wait for the political conditions to change before we begin building families based on

consent or before we assert our right to home educate with respect
for children's autonomy. Blankertz' analysis follows a very specific
political line and he perhaps underestimates the extent to which
people have the choice to opt out of this system within the privacy
of family units or alternative communities. The system of free state
provision of education is one that has enormous costs in terms of
liberty, but it is not as compulsory as it might appear. Blankertz'
case against compulsory, free state education is a strong one:

> "*Compulsory schooling is, whatever its specific contents or
> methods, the ultimate demonstration of State ownership of the
> children's bodies and of the parents' souls. Coercive parental
> control is sanctioned by the State, but the State denies or
> limits parents' freedom to choose the schooling. This traps the
> parents psychologically: Being in reality powerless in this
> respect, they can only continue to enjoy the feeling of power
> over the child by identifying with the State's decisions. Thus
> they grant the sanction of the victim.*
>
> "*The children are in a similar position: They are powerless
> but their impulse of rebellion is checked by their love of the
> parents. The children know, or at least feel, that school is
> compulsory. But because the parents are trapped into
> submitting to the State they act as if they want the children to
> go to school. Thus, any rebellion against State education is
> directed against the loved parents, not against the real
> aggressor, the State.*"
>
> (Blankertz, *The Manufacture of Subjection:*
> *A Critique of Compulsory State Education*)

The fact is, however, that school is not compulsory and parents who
coerce their children into going to school against their will are
simply hiding behind a state machine when they tell their children
that 'they have to go to school'. Writing in *Free Range Education*,
home educating parent, Kay Day, describes in distressing detail the
battle with her son to force him to go to school.

> "*Every professional opinion was that we should, at all costs,
> continue to insist on his attendance. Although my instinct
> screamed inside me to keep him at home, I had been told that
> it was my legal responsibility, as his parent, to get him to
> school.*"

As things became more and more traumatic, Day was offered a
specialist unit and psychiatric 'help' for her son:

"Dutifully, and still believing in the benign intentions of the state education system, we attended both for a short while."

Day writes with moving clarity about finding that there is an alternative and also highlights the role of parents in compulsion with remarkable honesty:

"We quickly realised that part of his trauma had been our fault. Due to our ignorance about children and our acceptance of the rightness and authority of 'experts', we violated L. We used our greater numbers, our physical power and psychological bullying to force him to submit to a system of schooling that was destroying him."

(Kay Day, 'What Lloyd Did Next', in *Free Range Education*)

Day's analysis is correct. It is the state that has a certain agenda for education and which perpetrates this agenda **at any cost** to individual children, but it is parents who decide whether to hand their children over, against their will, to this agenda. We do not have to wait for political reform, financial riches or anything else in order to begin living consensual relationships with our children, in education as in every aspect of life.

He who pays the piper

Whether our critique of the educational system stems from a political discontent with modernization, globalisation and capitalism; from libertarian and ethical arguments about autonomy, or from a simple desire to take control of the education of our own children, money will play its part. If we choose 'free' education in the sense of having freedom over its content and philosophy, then we cannot avail ourselves of the 'free' state-provided education without expending massive amounts of creative energy to avoid the many hidden costs.

Home educating families find a range of ways to finance their choices whatever their particular skills, lifestyle and initial income. One parent, considering how home education had impacted on family finances, wrote:

"I was not earning money when we began Home Education. My partner was in a reasonably well paid but demanding, stressful job. Had we known about Home Education sooner (preferably at birth!) we could have made other choices with money and time...We had a nice home in an expensive country town...and a small safe garden....and asked my partner to consider starting a private practice...from home. It was

something he had always considered doing but seemed impossible financially. We cashed in endowment policies linked to our mortgage after selling our home for a lot more than we paid for it and re-located ourselves to a city, buying outright a much larger home with a big garden. The children realise other children have more expensive toys, videos, clothes etc., but at the moment...they prefer we have more time for them. They see other children's expensive things as compensation for not being home-educated and having two parents working (or whatever combination). They are old enough to remember the other lifestyle and compare and decide what is of value to them at this point in time.

"Family finance is discussed and how we could choose to spend/how we do spend what we have and this is a huge learning experience for all of us and we don't take money for granted as much."

However modest the costs of home educating can be made, the financial responsibility is enough to raise the question within the home education community of whether government funding should be sought for this alternative. There are home educators who wish to go down this route and who believe that funding could be gained with little or no compromise of freedom. I am not persuaded. It is my view that funding always brings conditions, and that the educational liberty enjoyed by home educators is, at least in part, safeguarded by remaining financially self-sufficient. Although there is no doubt that this makes it a more difficult choice for families on lower incomes, it does not make it an impossible choice. It does contribute enormously to home education remaining the truly positive and 'free' alternative - an idea I explore in chapter six.

A choice of payments
Nothing is free. We have a choice as families as to what we are willing to pay for our children's education. If we choose home education, then the finances are up to individual families and it is better that this remains the case. If we choose school, against our children's will, then the price will vary, depending on our creativity to take what we want from the system and our individual children, but it could be very high and it could be our children who are paying on our behalf, as we will explore in the following chapters.

Chapter three

The myth of 'what's best for you'

Other people's benevolence can sometimes be a very oppressive and manipulative thing, perhaps never more so than when it is a government acting in the perceived best interests of a group which has no voice in the matter. In this chapter, I want to examine the **social or welfare** costs of free compulsory education, including the rise of medical, psychological and civil liberty intervention into families under the guise of education.

Against civil liberties
The special rapporteur to the United Nations, in noting that compulsory, state-provided schooling could be seen as a violation of human rights (see chapter 1 above) is simply re-stating criticism that has been made before. At the beginning of the eighties, writers like John Holt were arguing that compulsory school attendance laws are an issue of civil liberty:

> *"...compulsory school attendance laws, in and of themselves seem to me to be a very serious infringement of the civil liberties of children and their parents..."*
> *(John Holt, Teach Your Own, p.12)*

Holt goes on to describe how the nature and form of record keeping, compulsory psychological testing, compulsory diagnoses of bogus diseases and syndromes and the infliction of punishments on the basis of often unconfirmed reports are all infringements of civil liberties which would not be tolerated against any other group in society and in which *"anything that could fairly be called 'due process'"* is patently denied. He continues:

> *"To return once more to compulsory school attendance in its barest form, you will surely agree that if the government told you that on one hundred and eighty days of the year, for six or more hours a day, you had to be at a particular place, and there do whatever people told you to do, you would feel that this was a gross violation of your civil liberties. The State, of course, justifies doing this to children as a matter of public*

> *policy, saying that only thus can it keep them from being*
> *ignorant and a burden on the State. But even if it were true*
> *that children are learning important things in schools, and that*
> *they could not learn them anywhere else, neither of which I*
> *admit, it does not allow the needs of public policy to become*
> *an excuse for violating the basic civil liberties of citizens..."*
>   (John Holt, *Teach Your Own*, p.13)

Twenty years later, the current government in the United Kingdom
still speaks of children's 'rights' to go to school without a trace of
irony, and is channeling resources into new legislation under the
Crime and Disorder Act to combat truancy. The logic is that
children have a right to be in school and the government apparently
see no contradiction in imposing such a 'right' against a child's
will. The Social Exclusion Unit reports that 15% of children are
reported by schools as truanting, although anonymous surveys of
children put this figure at at least 30%, with 10% of fifteen-year-
olds truanting weekly, and 2% of year 11 children truanting for
weeks at a time. The report noted that Traveler children are a high-
risk group in terms of truanting and comments:

> *"Many others may not even be registered at school."*

There is no recognition in the report that school registration is not
compulsory and that parents do not have a legal duty to inform
Local Education Authorities of their decision to home educate if
their children are not already registered at a school.

The report sites examples of good practice in response to truancy,
which are cause for civil liberty concern. In one scheme in Stoke-
on-Trent in 1994, shopkeepers agreed to challenge school-aged
children during school hours and to refuse to serve them, a practice
which would no doubt discriminate against any children not in
school for wholly legitimate (by the government's own definition)
reasons, including home educators. In another scheme in Bradford,
electronic paging of parents and truants was piloted. The
government aim in regard to truancy is to engender a culture of zero
tolerance. There is never any question of whether children have a
right to absent themselves from a place they have never agreed to
go in the first place. This is so when children are being severely
bullied, experiencing daily failure and humiliation, or simply do not
consent to the education they are being coerced to consume.

The common presumption that free state education is compulsory
and that children's rights are being violated if they do not attend

school has given rise to a culture in which children are routinely suspect. This has an impact on families who are legally exercising their right to choose home education, perhaps particularly so since the implementation of the Crime and Disorder Act and associated truancy sweeps. The guidelines to the Crime and Disorder Act (sections 4.20 and 4.21) make it very clear that home-educated children are not the target of truancy sweeps and should not be questioned beyond ascertaining that they are home-educated. The guidelines were in response to pressure exerted by the home education community as to their fears that their children would no longer be able to go about their lives without fear of unwarranted police intervention. Many home-educated children now carry 'truancy cards' produced by *Choice in Education* and drawn up by a home-educating father who is lawyer. The cards point out that the children are lawfully home-educated and should not be required to give their name and address, but simply allowed to go on their way.

Despite this vigilance, abuses are still reported by home educators. In one recent report, a police constable and educational welfare officer at a local shopping centre stopped a child of 14. The child explained that she was home-educated and this explanation was accepted. The constable, however, then persisted in asking for the child's name and address. The child explained that since the officer had no reason to believe that a crime was being committed, she was under no obligation to give this information, but the officer persisted until the child gave in. He also told the child that home-educated children are not allowed to be on the streets during school hours, a fact that is not only false and not contained in any law, but which is explicitly contradicted in the guidelines to the Act. Soon after the incident, the child's father found the officers and asked if they were engaged in a designated truancy sweep. They confirmed that they were. The police officer also confirmed that he had never seen the guidelines to the Act and was not aware of their existence. Other home educators, it should be noted, have had much more positive experiences of how this law is being implemented, but it is clear that an awareness of home education is far from universal.

In another incident, the Educational Welfare Officer accompanying the police constable demanded the child's name, insisting that if the family were telling the truth, she would be able to match their name and address against a list of home educators known to the LEA. Since home educators are under no legal obligation to inform LEAs of their intentions to home educate, and since it appears that the majority of home educators do not want or have relations with an

LEA, this was clearly false and, again, beyond the provisions of the Act. The existence of a mass system of compulsory free state education compromises the civil liberties not just of those children whose parents send them to school, but also has civil liberties implications for home educators and demands constant vigilance.

The decision to attend school or not is a matter of civil liberty and basic human rights. Recently the *Guardian* newspaper noted that children are the only people who are simply not consulted when it comes to the 'services' provided for them. In a culture that is increasingly adamant that client participation and consultation represents best practice, it is only children, the paper pointed out, who have 'no choice'. With this in mind, the newspaper launched an appeal for children to write in about 'the school they want'. Amongst a page of letters from teachers, many decrying the impossibility of their task, one letter from a home-educated child read:

> *"Children have no choice over their education, you tell us, but for as many as 150,000 home-educated children this isn't true. These children don't want any kind of school. School is a training ground for bullies and victims. School is a place where you learn what someone else has decided for you. School is a place where parents can leave their children for free, without taking responsibility for their education. Having a say in the type of building or the uniforms or even some small say in what is taught or how teaching is done won't make much difference. The choice that children need is whether to be there or not. If more parents realized or allowed it, children already have this choice.*

> *"I like to choose what and how to learn. I don't want to be in any place where my property can be confiscated (like Pokemon cards or CD players). For me, learning is about living. I learn from everything I do and I make choices all the time. Choices are what growing up is all about and the choices have to be real, not just a bit of consultation to make you feel better. Anything else is just like asking prisoners how they want the prison to be run. It might make it more tolerable, but it's still compulsory.*

> *"Home education doesn't give you the school you want, it gives you the education and life you want."*
>   (Tamsyn Fortune-Wood, *The Guardian*, 23.01.01.)

The fact that school is provided with a view to children's best interests does not morally justify the coercion involved. No other group, outside prisoners and those who are sectioned for serious mental health disorders, are treated with such sweeping disregard to their basic human autonomy. The assumption that their younger age renders them incapable of having a voice in their own lives is simply not supportable. As I have argued elsewhere:

"...best interest must be an intrinsic question of autonomy. It is not for the parent to decide that it is in the child's best interest to receive the so-called discipline of God or to follow what everyone else agrees on as 'common sense' or to live a life without sugar, plastic toys or TV as so called 'nature' intended.... No matter how convinced the parent is they still could be wrong....No matter how well a parent knows their child, and no matter how much they love their child, they are not their child." (Fortune-Wood, *Without Boundaries*, p.38)

The same is even truer of the State, which makes a generalised provision that can never take into account the individual needs and preferences of the child with any degree of accuracy. Not long ago it was argued that women were too morally and intellectually weak and irrational to be able to make significant decisions for themselves about their lives. It was self-evident that it would be ridiculous to give them such control and that to do so would be against their 'best interests' as defined by men. At other times, similar arguments have been applied to black people, racial minorities or subject peoples. Increasingly, such arguments are derided as shameful examples of human rights abuse and scorned as fallacy. We still persist, however, in believing that children could not possibly follow their intrinsic interests without becoming selfish, irrational anti-social monsters. There is simply no evidence that this would be the case. Already children raised with respect for their autonomy, home-educated in environments of mutual consent, following their own interests, defy this unwarranted caricature.

"...Parents acting out of what they perceive to be a child's best interests will expend resources less optimally, either giving too much or too little in any particular area. Parents do much better to stay within the role of trusted advisor; offering information, best theories and criticism without presuming that in the final analysis they can know best for another person.

"...Acting out of self-interest is often feared as being tantamount to acting badly; a license for abusive behaviour....We can't, ultimately, force someone to lead a moral life, but we can rationally convince children that a

moral life and a self- interested life are mutually inclusive because the argument will stand up for itself. Immoral acts tend towards not only harming others, but also to being self-destruction on some level."

(Fortune-Wood, *Without Boundaries*, pp.30-31)

This is not a glib manifesto for young people and children to run amuck through society, but a serious call to trust that children can reason, can know what is in their interest and, with parental engagement, support and assistance, can meet intrinsic educational goals which a state system can never hope to match in terms of resources, individual responsiveness or human respect. The true question that the enormous incidence of truancy raises is not how can we coerce children back into the institution, but how can we build a society where children can be architects of their own present and future, fully supported by the parents who are fundamentally responsible for their education?

From psychology to medication
This is not a question that is being widely asked, even as we move into a postmodern society where event-driven living, creativity and flexibility are increasingly required. Rather, education as an arm of the state has further retrenched its controlling position by spreading its jurisdiction.

Non-educational welfare concerns have increasingly become accepted as educational concerns. This is most apparent in the rise of disorders and syndromes that are attributed to children who find it difficult or impossible to fit into the school structure and so exhibit 'behavioural' problems. An enormous body of opinion exists to suggest that good education is dependent on acquiring the prerequisite behavioural traits, and that for some children such behavioural traits can be acquired only through interventions, both medical and psychological. Russell Barkley is amongst those who are convinced that 'disease' lies at the heart of educational functionality. He deals with 'attention deficit hyperactivity disorder' (ADHD):

"Within the past several years, however, those of us who study ADHD have begun to clarify its symptoms and causes and have found that it may have a genetic underpinning. Today's view of the basis of the condition is strikingly different from that of just a few years ago. We are finding that ADHD is not a disorder of attention per se, as had long been assumed. Rather it arises as a developmental failure in the brain

circuitry that underlies inhibition and self-control. This loss of self-control in turn impairs other important brain functions crucial for maintaining attention, including the ability to defer immediate rewards for later, greater gain."

Insisting that ADHD is a disease, Barkley goes on:

"Boys are at least three times as likely as girls to develop the disorder; indeed, some studies have found that boys with ADHD outnumber girls with the condition by nine to one, possibly because boys are genetically more prone to disorders of the nervous system. The behavior patterns that typify ADHD usually arise between the ages of three and five. Even so, the age of onset can vary widely: some children do not develop symptoms until late childhood or even early adolescence. Why their symptoms are delayed remains unclear."

Without ever considering whether this 'late onset' of ADHD might have some cultural basis in the coercion children experience in the school environment, Barkley goes on to posit that research into brain imaging (research which remains far from substantiated) suggests less activity in so called ADHD brains and so demonstrates a polygenic disorder. He does not consider the possibility that the dynamic brain might have less activity simply because of the environmental coercive stresses. He certainly does not consider the possibility that the 'brain imaging' is simply faulty data. Rather Barkley goes on:

"Which genes are defective? Perhaps those that dictate the way in which the brain dopamine, one of the chemicals known as neurotransmitters that convey messages from one nerve cell, or neuron, to another.

"How do the brain-structure and genetic defects observed in children with ADHD lead to the characteristic behaviors of the disorder? Ultimately, they might be found to underlie impaired behavioral inhibition and self-control, which I have concluded are the central deficits in ADHD."

Barkley later argues that:

" It is my assertion that the inattention, hyperactivity and impulsivity of children with ADHD are caused by their failure to be guided by internal instructions and by their inability to curb their own inappropriate behaviors."

He then prescribes a combination of Ritalin, antidepressants and:

> *"treatment for ADHD should include training parents and teachers in specific and more effective methods for managing the behavioral problems of children with the disorder. Such methods involve making the consequences of a child's actions more frequent and immediate and increasing the external use of prompts and cues about rules and time intervals. Parents and teachers must aid children with ADHD by anticipating events for them, breaking future tasks down into smaller and more immediate steps, and using artificial immediate rewards. All these steps serve to externalize time, rules and consequences as a replacement for the weak internal forms of information, rules and motivation of children with ADHD."*

He concludes:

> *"There is no cure for ADHD, but much more is now known about effectively coping with and managing this persistent and troubling developmental disorder. The day is not far off when genetic testing for ADHD may become available and more specialized medications may be designed to counter the specific genetic deficits of the children who suffer from it."*
> (Barkley, *ADHD*)

Although diagnosing and prescribing continue to be more common features of many children's school lives, there are voices of caution raised. Baughaman, quoting the research of Ken Jacobson who made observations of English school children, considers that there is no objective difference in the behaviours of so called 'normal' and ADHD children, but rather the difference is of perception and is culturally specific. He contends that no real biological, numerological or genetic bases have been found to support ADHD as disease and concludes:

> *"This is the new 'discipline'. It works for psychiatry. It works for their controlling partner - the pharmaceutical industry."*
> (Baughaman, *Still Seeking ADHD*)

Such voices of protest and warning are no more articulately expressed than by Thomas Szasz. In an interview with Thomas Szasz, Randall Wyatt raises the possibility that certain behavioural traits are in fact treatable diseases with biological or genetic causes. Wyatt asked:

> *"Psychiatrists, of course, don't want to be pushed out of the picture. They want to hold on to schizophrenia as long as they*

*can, and now depression and gambling, and drug abuse, and
so on, are proposed as biological or genetically determined.
Everything is thought to have a genetic marker, perhaps even
normality. What do you make of this?"*

To which Szasz replied:

*"I hardly know what to say about this silliness. Unless a
person understands the history of psychiatry and something
about semantics, it's very difficult to deal with this. Diagnoses
are NOT diseases. Period. Psychiatrists have had some very
famous diseases for which they have never apologized, the two
most obvious ones being masturbation and homosexuality.
People with these so-called "diseases" were tortured by
psychiatrists - for hundreds of years. Children were tortured
by anti-masturbation treatments. Homosexuals were
incarcerated and tortured by psychiatrists. Now all that is
conveniently forgotten, while psychiatrists invent new diseases,
like the ones you mentioned. The war on drugs is the current
psychiatric-judicial pogrom. And so is the war on children
called 'hyperactive', poisoned in schools with the illegal street
drug called 'speed', which, when called 'Ritalin', is a miracle
cure for them."*

(Wyatt and Szasz Interview, www.psychotheraopistresources.com)

It is certainly the case that those children whose behaviour is
particularly troublesome in the classroom environment, are not only
given the ADHD label, but are also medicated as part of their
educational experience. Szasz raises the alarm when he refers to
ADHD as :

"...our present-day epidemic of mental illness..."

comparable to:

*"...the nineteenth-century epidemic of mental illness called
"masturbatory insanity."*

Szasz notes that he is not surprised by the enormous rate of increase
in drugs prescribed to very young children:

*"In February, a group of physicians writing in the Journal of
the American Medical Association reported that the use of
'psychotropic medications prescribed for preschoolers
increased dramatically between 1991 and 1995.' About twice
as many children between the ages of 2 and 4 were given
Ritalin, Prozac, and other so-called psychotropic drugs at the
end of that period as at the beginning of it."*

He goes on:

> *"To grasp the enormity of the stupidity that informs these so-called diagnoses, we must be clear about the difference between a diagnosis and a disease.*
>
> *"...The concept of diagnosis is contingent on the concept of disease. Diagnosis is the name of a disease, just as, say, violet is the name of a flower. For example, the term 'diabetes' names a type of abnormal glucose metabolism. The disease qua somatic pathology - literal disease - is the abnormal metabolism; the diagnosis, 'diabetes', is its name...Unless we keep in mind that diseases are facts of nature, whereas diagnoses are artifacts constructed by human beings, and that the core meaning of the term 'disease' is lesion, we forfeit the possibility of understanding the uses and abuses of the term 'diagnosis'.*
>
> *"Unlike bodily illnesses, mental illnesses are diagnosed by finding unwanted behaviors in persons or by attributing such behaviors to them. Bodily illnesses - say, cancer or diabetes - are located in bodies; mental illnesses - say, kleptomania or schizophrenia - are located in social contexts. Robinson Crusoe could suffer from cancer, but not from kleptomania.*
>
> *"The diagnosis of a mental illness validates its own disease status. Disease qua psychopathology cannot be asymptomatic and changing the nosology can change disease into non-disease and vice versa (for example, homosexuality into civil right and smoking into substance abuse). Mental diseases are diagnoses, not diseases. Conversely, psychiatric diagnoses (however constructed) are, by definition, mental diseases (or 'disorders', to use the mental health professionals' preferred weasel word).*

(Szasz, Thomas S., *Chemical Straitjackets for Children*, Copyright 2001, The Foundation for Economic Education)

Szasz reminds us that to understand the tactical rather than descriptive uses of terms such as 'ill' and 'patient', we must ask ourselves, 'Who gains by it?' He proposes that man's character is such that no man undertakes crimes without hope of gain.

> *"Mutatis mutandis, no man asserts that he or someone else has an illness without hope of gain. The goods that a person gains from asserting such a claim range from securing medical help for himself to justifying controlling the Other by defining coercion as cure. Consider the evidence:*

"The disease of masturbation affected mainly children; so does the disease of hyperactivity. The disease of masturbation pained parents, teachers, and other adults, not the denominated patients; the disease of hyperactivity pains and does not pain the same persons, respectively. The disease of masturbation was treated with physical restraints forcibly imposed on the bodies of children; the disease of hyperactivity is treated with chemical restraints forcibly introduced into the bodies of children.

"The disease of masturbation was the favorite diagnosis of doctors and parents dealing with troublesome children in the nineteenth century; attention deficit hyperactivity disorder is the favorite diagnosis of doctors and parents dealing with troublesome children today.

"Belief in masturbatory insanity was, as I emphasized, not an innocent error. Neither is belief in ADHD. Each belief is a manifestation of the adults' annoyance by certain ordinary childhood activities, their efforts to control or eliminate the activities to allay their own discomfort, and the medical profession's willingness to diagnose disturbing childhood behaviors, thus medicalizing and justifying the domestication of children by drugs defined as therapeutic.

"Formerly, quacks had fake cures for real diseases; now, they claim to have real cures for fake diseases".
(Szasz, Thomas S., *Chemical Straitjackets for Children,* Copyright 2001, The Foundation for Economic Education)

Within schools, more and more children whose individuality does not fit them to an increasingly restrictive environment are being diagnosed and 'treated'. The costs are enormous: the economic cost to the taxpayers who fund this part of the 'health' service; the special educational resources committed to forcing children to fit into the system; not to mention the horrendous personal costs, which have the spin-off of massive social costs. I have previously argued that coercion damages thinking ability and rationality:

"When we choose coercion over finding a common preference, we not only loose the possibility of new knowledge being created, but also risk impairing our ability to think, learn, and solve problems. In situations where there is a problem to be solved, coerced children will abandon the attempt to creatively problem solve, knowing it to be futile since ultimately the solution will be imposed by the adults. Learning does not take place and creativity is trampled. Children need to have

successful experiences of finding solutions and having control
over their own lives. Coercion replaces this experience with
feelings of powerlessness, resentment, and frustration, adding
painful feelings to areas of thinking and another blockage to
rational thinking. Coercion helps to convince children that life
is difficult, that getting what one wants is next to impossible
and that doing things one hates in inevitable; non-coercion
creates flexible thinkers who see that they can control their
lives, and develop lives which they want to live."
(Fortune-Wood, *Without Boundaries*, p.22)

Following the philosophy of *Taking Children Seriously*, it is my
contention that intrinsic learning and coercion are inimical. A
coercive school system, with the collusion of parents and the
backing of educational, welfare, medical and government
professionals, has a fixed idea of what learning children must
achieve. This agenda sabotages attempts to pursue unsanctioned
learning for much of the children's time. Faced with this frustration,
children may abandon their attempts to satisfy their intrinsic
motivation to learn what matters to them, or develop a range of
sophisticated coping strategies. Some of these strategies will draw
unwanted attention, resulting in diagnosis and treatment that risks
the effect of a crushing of the child's preferences, creativity and
motivation. Such children are likely to become adults hardly aware
of their own preferences for their lives, and who are convinced that
even if they know what they want, they cannot have it.

"People sometimes object that they know of many children
whose parents employ coercion and many adults who were
coerced as children who are nevertheless bright, successful,
intelligent people. This might be true, but it does not mean that
the coercion they experienced did no damage.

"It might be that the bright, intelligent person is none-the-less
very poor at forming relationships or has irrational thinking
difficulties when it comes to washing dishes or can't bear to be
disagreed with. Some people may be much more resilient to
the effects of coercion than others, but this does not justify
coercion. As parents, we can't predict what damage any
particular act of coercion will do. What we can predict is that
at some point, in some areas and to some degree, coercion will
cause thinking damage. We can also cogently hold that all
coercion has the potential to cause damage. Why damage our
children? The usual reason is that we are committing some
minor bad for some greater good; that we are limiting our

children's preferences out of their own best interests. This
reasoning is false..."
(Fortune-Wood, *Without Boundaries*, pp.23-24)

The monolithic system of 'free' compulsory state education has
done a great deal to convince us that children who are perceived as
'square pegs' are being helped if they are treated in such a way that
they will eventually fit into round holes. Is this true? Is it the
children who are faulty, or is it that the system, which requires all
children to imbibe an entire national curriculum in a set order
regardless of its intrinsic interest to individuals, is wasteful,
inefficient and oppressive? Are the children mentally ill or is the
system a poor fit for the vast wealth of individual learning styles
and creativity that exist in our children? Are we so afraid of human
nature and so mistrusting of children in particular that we believe
that without a bland, one-size-fits-all curriculum we will fall into a
state of uneducated chaos? Individual children are being consigned
to a medicated hell to satiate this pessimism and fearfulness. It is
not only the children, but, ultimately, all of us who lose by this
system. Children are not products and they do not exist to fulfil a
list of required functions for society. If we nurture children to
pursue intrinsic motivation and self-fulfillment, the spin-offs for
both individual and society at large will be optimally creative and
beneficial.

"The goal of parenting (or education) is not to control, but to
facilitate the child in self-maximising and following their
intrinsic motivation. This goal relies on the assumptions that
children are rational, creative, trustworthy and autonomous
human beings living in environments where they have
sufficient information to be able to make good decisions for
themselves by their own lights.

"Self-interest is, in fact, the only way to guarantee that those
activities engaged in and decisions made are the right ones for
any particular individual's learning, growth and well-being. If
children rely on parental perceptions of what is right for them,
there is actually no way of guaranteeing that the individual
child's unique self will be best served. This is because the
parents are likely to be working on a preconceived agenda of
what is best for children in general or from their own
perceptions of the child, which, whilst they might be good
approximations, can never be equal to the child's self-
knowledge. Children whose intrinsic motivations are being
followed and whose self-interest is being helped and facilitated

will experience a greater satisfaction from life, a greater belief in their own ability to control their lives and an increase in well being and self-motivation."
(Fortune-Wood, *Without Boundaries,* p.30)

It is not in anyone's best interests that children should be forced to fit into a homogenous system at any price. It is a tragic waste of real creativity and learning potential, one that does not need to happen when schooling is not compulsory.

Home education is not a welfare issue

Many welfare concerns are not the proper territory of education. In terms of home-based education, it is vital to the integrity of the learning that welfare and education be seen as separate issues. With this in mind, there need to be boundaries around the intrusion of assessment into the provision of home-based education. It should be safe to assume that both parents and professionals have the best interests of children at heart. Sadly, this may not always be the case. Professionals can be over-zealous; both from a concern that to not be so would be a failure of care, and from a fear of subsequent negative come-back if serious problems come to light by some other route. Despite this, it needs to be clearly understood that Local Education Authority officers have a duty in terms of education, not welfare (unless there are real grounds for concerns that any citizen should take seriously). In particular, they have a responsibility, if it appears to them that there is no educational provision or, in practice, if they make informal inquiries, to be satisfied that parents are discharging their duty to educate their children according to age, ability and aptitude.

All statutory bodies, as well as all concerned and responsible citizens, have the duty to be alert for signs of real abuse, but this is a far cry from imagining that the pursuit of home-based education in and of itself is a *prima facie* signal of possible abuse. LEA officers, in seeking to make inquiries about the suitability of education, have no right of access to the children or the premises of home educating families. Families can and do choose ways of giving evidence that involve neither access to their homes nor to their children. This in itself should not be a cause for any alarm. Within the home educating community, there is a diverse range with valid educational and philosophical reasons for such choice, depending on particular educational styles and assumptions. It is not only families who 'have something to hide' that do not opt for home visits. Families who have a particular view of their children's privacy or follow a particular kind of autonomous education or have particular religious views or simply prefer other means of giving evidence more to their taste and convenience, will all routinely opt not to have home visits. It is the essence of a tolerant liberal democracy that we respect people's freedom to present evidence in any reasonable form and do not form unsubstantiated views as to why they might make particular choices.

Some professionals might still feel uneasy with this stance, but would have to ask themselves whether, even if one LEA could legally insist on home visits with the children present, would such visits consistently or even regularly 'save' abused children? It is quite possible that visits conducted with welfare rather than education in mind would result in an increase in trauma and wrongful suspicion, especially in families following quite legitimate alternative life-styles, or where families do not 'fit' with the particular expectations or prejudices of individual Educational Welfare Officers.

Stories of patent injustice already exist amongst the home educating community. For example, a mother having social services brought in and enduring the trauma of investigation simply because she was too ill to do much cleaning while pregnant! We all know that abuse can take place in households that are spotlessly clean or where parents can pleasantly charm any stranger, including experienced professionals. We also know that children virtually never disclose to strangers (unless there is some anonymity as with phone lines). Even if children had their ten minutes alone with a very friendly EWO, they are still unlikely to disclose anything of import. In the absence of clear disclosures of abuse, it would then fall to pressurized Educational Welfare Officers to 'spot' something. Are homes where children wear pyjamas at 10:30 in the morning, or where no one remembers to open the curtains some days, 'suspicious'? Some lifestyles might seem strange, but they are not necessarily abusive; the spectrum is quite enormous. We also have to hold in mind that the alternative to these 'strange' homes is institutional care, which has its own phenomenal statistics of abuse and high rates of tragic outcomes (prostitution, substance abuse, criminality, etc.).

There is a danger that if we were to expect the home educating community to accept visits on welfare grounds, they would then have to start worrying about conforming their lifestyles to the visits; not in order to hide abuse, but simply in order to be seen as 'normal'.

Advising home educators to give evidence via home visits to appease general concerns over welfare when there are no specific indicators for such concerns is opening up home-based educators to a whole range of spurious problems which other members of society are not subject to.

Home education is not a welfare issue *per se*. Those with a genuine remit must be careful not to act beyond the legal parameters as matter of general policy. LEAs have to satisfy themselves of suitable education (if it appears that such an education might not be taking place or if it chooses to make informal inquiries) according to age, ability, aptitude and any special educational needs. It is for the home educating families to choose how to reply and to set out their definitions of what education is for their families. LEAs have no statutory duty to define education as a *prima facie* welfare concern.

The repost to this is always, 'But who will look out for those children who are being abused?', with the underlying assumption that if children are not within the institutional framework of school, then anything could be happening to them. LEAs can reassure themselves that the prospect of a home-educated child growing up and suing them for negligence looks like a very remote possibility. Grown up children who were in school have, so far, not been able to establish such an individual responsibility of LEAs towards school children. This is of a negative and somewhat cynical reason to not see home education as a welfare issue, but more positive and constructive reasons do exist.

It is simply not the case that children must be in some sort of institutional catchall to be safe. If we did have such a notion, then health visitors would have statutory access to homes. Clearly they do not, and the average parent would justifiably be horrified by the suggestion that a government agency should routinely visit the homes of all under-fives to ensure that they are not being abused. It should also be noted that many children go through the whole of their school life with abuse undetected, or grow up in government-funded care homes with abuse undetected. Having some institution with an overview of the child is no guarantee. Disclosure is a very elusive state. Its rise has been linked more with the anonymity of charities like *Child Line* or with adults after-the-event disclosures, than with the majority of children being in institutions for large parts of each day.

We would also have to consider what kind of welfare checks would actually be needed to pick up serious abuse in home educating households? Relying on rapidly formed impressions, except in the most extreme of circumstances, is simply not good enough. Picking up on peripheral issues (such as hazards on the stairs, smoke in the air, a dirty toilet etc.) is clearly discriminatory because these checks are not made on non-home educating homes. It is not enough to say that schools have to have health and safety checks; homes are not schools. Home education is a totally different form of education. Many parallels simply do not exist. It is not enough to say that it is because home-educated children spend more time in the home than school children; this may or may not be true. Home education is, in reality, home-based education, with much of the education taking place in libraries, museums, streets, parks and so on. If we were to concede that welfare checks on home-educated children are valid, then we would have to allow welfare checks of sufficient scope to really catch the serious cases. What would that mean? Compulsory interviews with psychologists? Full body examinations, including genital inspection? Would any of this be consistent with the tolerant liberal democracy in which we live? Could such an abuse of civil liberties ever be out-balanced by the outside possibility of rarely revealing a real case of abuse? Furthermore, what would be the equally, if not more, abusive consequences to the home-educated children enduring the immense trauma of such routine invasion to absolutely no purpose or benefit in the vast majority of cases? Such draconian measures are neither tolerable not justifiable.

This leaves the uncomfortable possibility that a very few home-educated children will be abused and that this abuse will go undetected. This is also true of many schooled or pre-schooled children. This sad fact has never justified any government to imagine it should impose sweeping welfare checks of the level of intrusion that would be needed to make all abuse impossible. There are very good civil liberty reasons for the absence of such policies. The real answer is that there is no foolproof system unless every sector of the community gives up all privacy and civil liberties in this area. Even if this where to happen, we would simply have a new form of abuse in the form of traumatic abuse checks. We are left with an imperfect society, certainly, but one in which the home education community presents no *prima facie* welfare concern. There are no supportable reasons to discriminate against it on these grounds as a matter of general policy.

Secrecy is the key to abuse, but contrary to popular conceptions, withdrawing children from school is a fairly high-profile activity. Abused children are more likely to disappear from the system than to make the pro-active transition from school-based education to elective home-based education. Never sending children to school might, conceivably, be a means of hiding, but submitting families who are known to their LEAs to welfare checks is a totally ineffective way of helping children in families who are unknown to their LEAs. This is not, however, an argument for the compulsory registration of home educating families with local education authorities (a requirement that does not currently exist). Families who are determined to hide could still attempt and often succeed in doing so and it would still have to be borne in mind that cases of 'hiding' will, most often, not signal abuse, but religious or philosophical grounds for maintaining educational privacy.

We have a national consensus that intrusive checks for abuse, such as stressful interviews or body searches on all children, are not an acceptable price to pay for the minimal extra detection that could arise. Since only these illegal and intrusive checks would significantly increase detection rates in the home education community, it would seem pointless to expect home educators to submit to lesser discriminatory checks that will actually have little or no effect or even produce false accusations.

Autonomous welfare
Without the burdens of intrusive and unnecessary welfare checks and without the need to force children who present themselves differently into narrow molds of conformity and functionality, home-educated children can enjoy a wide latitude in having their best interests met. Wherever autonomy is promoted, children's 'own good', by their own lights rather than some external agenda, follows.

Chapter four

The cost of conformity

The cost to individuals of being required to conform to institutionalised systems, which I explored in chapter three above, are widely pervasive. In this chapter I will go on to expand upon other aspects of these costs. Any state-controlled system of education necessarily tends towards a conformity culture which ill serves the needs of individuals and ultimately ill serves the nurturing of creativity in society. I want to argue that such conformity carries a high probability of severe **emotional** and **thinking** costs for the individual. These costs are well illustrated in examples of bullying and labelling. I will argue that the coercion damage and the attack on individuality are both inimical to free society and a tragic waste of human resources.

The 'dictated curriculum'
The content of what is taught in schools is increasingly homogenized. The advent of literacy and numeracy hours have effectively taken over large swathes of the curriculum, with literacy hours being structured according to an imposed, external programme almost down to the minute. This regulation of curriculum content itself militates against individualised learning; more fundamentally, the hidden curriculum conspires to ensure that what is taught is, above all else, conformity. John Taylor Gatto, formerly 'teacher of the year' in New York, has cogently argued this:

"What I teach is school, and I win awards doing it. ... Teaching means many different things, but six lessons are common to schoolteaching from Harlem to Hollywood. You pay for these lessons in more ways than you can imagine, so you might as well know what they are:

*"The **first** lesson I teach is: 'Stay in the class where you belong'. I don't know who decides that my kids belong there but that's not my business. The children are numbered so that if any get away they can be returned...*

"The second lesson I teach kids is to turn on and off like a light switch. I demand that they become totally involved in my lessons, jumping up and down in their seats with anticipation, competing vigorously with each other for my favor. But when the bell rings I insist that they drop the work at once and proceed quickly to the next work station. Nothing important is ever finished in my class, nor in any other class I know of.

"The lesson of bells is that no work is worth finishing....

*"The **third** lesson I teach you is to surrender your will to a predestined chain of command. Rights may be granted or withheld, by authority, without appeal...My judgments come thick and fast, because individuality is trying constantly to assert itself in my classroom. Individuality is a curse to all systems of classification....*

*"The **fourth** lesson I teach is that only I determine what curriculum you will study (rather, I enforce decisions transmitted by the people who pay me)....*

"Bad kids fight against this, of course, trying openly or covertly to make decisions for themselves about what they will learn. How can we allow that and survive as schoolteachers? Fortunately there are procedures to break the will of those who resist.

*"In **lesson five** I teach that your self-respect should depend on an observer's measure of your worth. My kids are constantly evaluated and judged....*

"Self-evaluation - the staple of every major philosophical system that ever appeared on the planet - is never a factor in these things.

*"In **lesson six** I teach children that they are being watched. I keep each student under constant surveillance and so do my colleagues....Students are encouraged to tattle on each other, even to tattle on their parents. Of course I encourage parents to file their own child's waywardness, too.*

"I assign 'homework' so that this surveillance extends into the household, where students might otherwise use the time to learn something unauthorized...The lesson of constant surveillance is that no one can be trusted, that privacy is not legitimate."

(Gatto, J.T. (1991) *The Six-Lesson Schoolteacher*)

At this point, Gatto gives an explanation as to why this anti-educational system persists. Over time the system erodes the imagination of those who go through it and emerge at the other end:

> *"It is the great triumph of schooling that among even the best of my fellow teachers, and among even the best parents, there is only a small number who can imagine a different way to do things....*
>
> *"It only takes about 50 contact hours to transmit basic literacy and math skills well enough that kids can be self-teachers from then on. The cry for 'basic skills' practice is a smokescreen behind which schools pre-empt the time of children for twelve years and teach them the six lessons I've just taught you."*
>
> (Gatto, J.T. (1991) *The Six-Lesson Schoolteacher*)

Children who are compelled to take part in this environment of conformity are put under enormous personal pressure. Those who do not conform are 'bad' and/or 'dysfunctional'; they might be diagnosed and treated, or they might become subject to various trends in behaviour modification. If this does not achieve the required results, then it is likely that the net of compulsory conformity will be cast more widely; the whole family may be put under scrutiny and subjected to family therapy or welfare intervention. The more the system feels threatened, the more aggressive the intervention. The child is left knowing, in no uncertain terms, that she is responsible for failing her parents, that she is causing trouble and that there is something severely wrong with her. The parents, for their part, quickly understand that they are the shameful producers of the wrong sort of child-product; they are bad or failing parents. In an article, *Public School Pandemonium: my experience as a public school teacher*, Rachel Baxter, quoting Isabel Patterson (*The God of the Machine*) posits that:

> *"A tax-supported, compulsory educational system is the complete model of the totalitarian state."*

She goes on to compare children in schools to the android wives in the film *The Stepford Wives*:

> *"...nothing...prepared me for the harsh reality of what I witnessed being done to kids in the public schools.*
>
> *"And like Ross's character, I was stunned that nobody - teachers, parents, and administrators - thought anything was wrong ...Everywhere I turned, kids were subjected to some sort of emotional, physical, intellectual, or spiritual*

carnage...In fact, the system was bent on destroying any uniqueness, intellectual curiosity, or self-discovery that these kids brought with them into the school....

"The system is specifically designed to chip away, piece by piece, a child's inherent right to develop into an independent-minded, psychologically aware, autonomous human being.

"...Many times I'd be in the middle of a discussion or project with a child and a bell would blast so loud, I'd have to cover my ears. Everyone else would be oblivious to the intrusion and move to another place - like rats in a cage."

Baxter goes on to list examples of how the system acts against individuality and self esteem:

"Children being forced to waste an inordinate amount of time waiting. They wait for other kids to finish their work; for recess; to go in after recess; for lunch; to go in after lunch; to answer a question; to ask a question; to go to the bathroom; to get on the bus; to take roll. They learn that wasting precious time is normal. They do not learn how to manage time for themselves.

"They learn to shut down their own natural joy of learning for its intrinsic rewards; and instead, perform like circus animals in order to get rewards.

"Legally drugging kids with amphetamines or other psychotropic medications in order to control behavior. This is medicalizing and drugging normal childhood behaviors to control kids...

"Kids learn that they have no rights with respect to their physical and intellectual well-being.

"Preventing healthy, meaningful relationships by artificially fragmenting time, separating younger kids from the older; 'slower' from the 'quicker'; popular from unpopular; competing with other students for teachers' attention; or teachers and administrators functioning as guards instead of caring mentors...They do not learn to effectively socialize with varying age groups or intellectual abilities.

"There is no time for the child to discover what he or she loves. All time is taken up by what others deem to be useful or appropriate...Kids being constantly told: 'You need to learn this because you may use it when you're an adult'. Or: 'Follow

directions without questioning because when you have a job, your boss is going to expect you to do as you are told'. The student learns that for the rest of her life, she'll be a subordinant - always being told what to do - never being the boss herself. She learns that the present moment means nothing other than to provide for some obscure time or reason in the future."

(Rachel Baxter, *Public School Pandemonium: my experience as a public school teacher*)

Human creativity and intrinsic motivation is very powerful. When it is systematically and persistently thwarted, it is not always predictable how individuals will react. Some will find that they can meet the school agenda with relative ease; others will find it difficult, but become passive and crushed quite quickly. Others will become variously confused, frustrated or angry and exhibit behaviours that the system must do all in its power to suppress.

Blaming the victim

Bullying is fast becoming one of the major reasons for withdrawal of children from state schools. Although home education begins with negative motivations in these cases, its positive impact soon becomes increasingly apparent. It is not easy to have a gracious perception of the apparent seven-year-old thug who has knocked your six-year-old's teeth out, but the bullies themselves are deeply unhappy children for whom the system does not work. If these children were able to act out of optimal self-interest by their own lights, then they would not be acting immorally. Harming others involves giving up rights and losing the possibility of being treated seriously by others. Even very young children know this on some level and act with aggression not because it will get them the good that they want out of life, but because they are unable to think clearly, hampered by coercion and the irrationality it engenders. Left to fend for themselves in an environment that pins children down when they want to expend energy; that dictates when and what they will learn and do, even to the point of needing permission to go to the toilet; that models a 'might is right' hierarchy; that distrusts the personal motivation of children and that measures out self esteem by your latest test score, it is hardly surprising that some children become aggressive towards their fellow inmates. It is certainly immoral for children to bully other children, but, fundamentally, is it children or the system that is intrinsically bad?

It is not only the perpetrators of aggression who are liable to be labelled and treated as misfits who need to learn true conformity. The children who find themselves bullied are just as likely to be perceived as faulty products, regularly accused of playing their role in inviting violence. Amongst home educators, there are many horrific stories of how children who have been bullied have themselves been perceived as needing 'modification'. It is not uncommon for bullied children to be accused of having a 'victim mentality' or for their family to be suspected of being in some sense dysfunctional and in need of treatment to enable the child to conform and fit without 'attracting' aggression. Children who are deeply miserable within the school environment, often children who are also being bullied, might become highly resistant to entering the environment that they fear and hate. This is not seen as a normal response, but instead is regarded as a kind of pathology with the label 'school phobia' neatly attached.

A phobia is, by definition, an irrational response. Having conducted research amongst home educators using an internet mailing list, Mike Fortune-Wood noted that not only is school phobia viewed as a psychological disorder caused by anxiety, but is also often seen as a disorder arising not from anxiety over school itself, but because there is some other problem at home. He writes,

> "From the evidence sent to me by parents, it appears that schools will often play down or even ignore problems relating to school. For example parents reported: 'He also came home with loads of bruises and was actually held down in the playground and stamped on and came home with a broken nose !!!!! None of which the school told me about. One day another mother approached me and told me that she had been helping out in school and that K had been near hysterical for over an hour. The school had not approached me at all.'

> "Another: 'He was dragged around the playground and eventually stripped naked. We found out about the incident from the child, not the school. When we confronted the head about this bullying we were told that it was not bullying but harassment. It was inferred that we were making a fuss.'

> "The professionals then go on to attempt to accuse the parents of being behind the problem. One parent reported: 'I have had Munchausen's by proxy bandied at me, been labelled neurotic, over-anxious, accused of loving B too much, of playing into his hands and so on. The emotional battering has left me punch drunk'.

> "The definition goes on to say: 'In contrast to normal school

anxieties, which tend to alleviate with time, school phobia often requires psychotherapy. The longer the time away from school, the worse the problem often becomes. It is, therefore, important to treat it aggressively, with the most immediate goal being to get the child back into the classroom as soon as possible.'

"The recommended treatment is aggressive and aimed rather surprisingly not at dealing with the child's needs but at the extraneously determined goal of returning the child to school. The problem with this is that there appears to be little or no recognition of the possibility that the child's anxiety is real, rather than irrational. The child's anxiety over school is rather incoherently attributed to the home, a place s/he would apparently prefer to be than with the school, the place the child wants to avoid being. One family described it thus: 'Her self-confidence evaporated. Wouldn't anyone sane avoid this type of experience? Such avoidance is an indication of sanity and good sense!'

"According to the accepted definition therefore the school and the education system bears no responsibility for school phobia which is the entire fault of the parents who are probably alcoholic, undergoing marital conflict, anxiety or depression.

"In the UK the method of 'treatment' varies quite widely but reports from a number of home educating parents suggest that strategies include threatening the child with their parents imprisonment or fining for their child's nonattendance of school."

Mike Fortune-Wood goes on to site a range of pressures brought to bear on parents to force their children to attend, noting:

"This leads parents into a 'catch 22' situation. When faced with problems with their child's schooling, parents are left with three choices. They can either leave the problem entirely to the school to solve, take up their children's cause and assist their child find a solution by advocating for him or her with the school authorities or actively support whatever action the LEA advocates.

"If a parent leaves it to the school then the parent is at real risk of being thought of as an uncaring parent, taken to court for allowing the child to truant and could therefore realistically expect to be fined up to several thousands of pounds. And perhaps subjected to a parental guidance order

by the courts.

"If, on the other hand, the parent advocates the child's view then the parent is marked down as over-anxious him or her self and therefore the probable cause of the anxiety in the first place. Again with this option they may find that they will be subjected to court action....

"The only action open to the parent is to agree with the professionals, regardless of their own view and actively force the child to attend school. Dr. Monk of the University of Pittsburgh Medical Centre says that the parent must: 'Explain why children must go to school'.

"And: 'Firmly explain that staying home from school is not an option'. This is a common reaction among educational advisors and educational psychologists in this country also, even though it is legally incorrect (as it is in Pittsburgh).

"Parents describe how their relationship with their children is damaged by this advice. 'When we had counsellors, psychologists etc. on the case, I know that he felt himself that there was something terribly wrong with him [our child]. We'd all convinced ourselves that he had some dreadful mental problem. Now we are on our own, we treat him like the normal intelligent person that he is - and he has come to realise that he is a perfectly normal person. During this entire horrible period our son became withdrawn and difficult. Life was so stressful for the whole family...Severing links with all the professionals (well meaning though they were) lifted a great weight from our shoulders. He became a different person and, though we've had good days and bad he has approached his studies fairly well. We have begun to feel 'normal' again.... The change in him has been remarkable and his confidence is slowly growing.'

"The professional community, particularly educational psych-ologists, have, I believe, sold out to the idea that the only place where education can take place is the school and that all other considerations, including the child's welfare, should be put firmly into second place to this notion...The profession as a whole is dominated by those with a vested interest not to question this assumption since so many educational psychiatrists are employed by the educational establishment. I believe that this exhibits professional cowardice and a stunning lack of imagination.

"Behind all of this lies a problem endemic in our society.

Children's voices are simply not heard. They are systematically ignored, patronised and marginalised. Labelling children who cannot stand the idea of going to a place inappropriate to their needs as irrational and exhibiting underlying psychological disorders is just another way of not taking children seriously. This needs to stop. We must start listening to children."

(Fortune-Wood, M.C., *School Phobia*)

The call to start listening to children goes to the heart of the problem. Criticisms of the school and of the professionals routinely coercing children into schools against their will are certainly germane, but parents themselves can end the distress with a single letter of de-registration. Not all schools refuse to entertain the notion that the child may be reacting quite rationally to an inappropriate environment, especially where bullying is the trigger for school refusal. Even with the advent of school bullying policies, however, and the constant input of support agencies like *Kidscape* and *Bullying Online*, the duty of care that schools owe children is still routinely undermined by school officials who simply feel inadequate to the problem and so are more likely to dismiss allegations or focus on the bullied child as a 'provocative victim'. This is certainly the impression gained from reading the email extracts of *Bullying Online*'s support site, for example:

"My seven-year-old son is experiencing problems with another boy who regularly hits and kicks him. We have approached the school on numerous occasions. The last meeting with the head resulted in me being told that if I didn't like her discipline procedures I should move my son."

"I've been told that I'm over-reacting and that my son aged 13 isn't being bullied, it's mostly horseplay and he's too sensitive and needs to recognise the difference. I'm quite fed up and thinking about moving him to another school."

"My daughter is 11 and has been bullied mentally by the same girl for three years. I have mentioned it to the school many times, it stops for a while then starts again. The teacher asked my daughter this morning if she was sure this was happening or if she was imagining it. I was very upset."

"The bullying is very subtle and her confidence is being chipped away. She has this girl shouting in her face and not letting her join in games as well and pinching her books. She doesn't eat, sleep or smile anymore and wants to leave school and never go back. We have a doctor's visit soon as I am so

worried about her. I'm afraid of making things worse by complaining again."

"My son who is nine has been bullied for a nearly a year and we don't know what to do next. We keep being told that he brings it on himself. I'm fed up with writing to the head."

"My daughter aged 10 is being bullied by a number of girls in her class. We have spoken to the head and staff many times. They say they cannot discipline the girls unless they have proof. They have picked several girls from the class, including some of the bullies to monitor the playground."

This is so upsetting that my daughter has insomnia and is afraid to go to school, she has become sullen and frustrated which is not like her. We have found that other girls are suffering bullying as well..."   (Bullying Online)

The site offers a considerable amount of reasoned and well-considered advice on systematically handling such issues, yet bullying remains endemic and for many children takes years to get any kind of resolution, if they ever get it at all. The site notes that the National Association of Head Teachers has issued guidelines, but also notes:

"Bullying Online is very disappointed and surprised that since the guidelines were issued to the Press on January 4 the NAHT no longer includes the clause 'the bullied individual must be supported' - while bullies are to be offered support."
(Bullying Online)

Bullying is another of the costs of having a free compulsory state system of education. Whilst children are not free to leave the school, school solutions to bullying will always be at best partial and insufficient.

Educating to the 'label'
Another severe and increasingly common aspect of the emotional costs of a homogenous monolithic system of free education comes in the form of burgeoning labels for pseudo-diseases that children are 'diagnosed' with, in order to shift the focus of failure away from the non-individually responsive institution and onto the individual. This is particularly the case with so-called hyperactivity disorders such as ADHD (Attention Deficit Hyperactivity Disorder) as was discussed in chapter 3 above. Another label that is becoming more commonly applied is 'Asperger's Syndrome', a supposedly lower

spectrum autistic tendency that now 'afflicts' increasing numbers of school children.

Two years ago, I had never heard of 'Asperger's Syndrome'. Suddenly, it is a 'condition', which seems to be proliferating in classrooms everywhere, amongst stressed young children who are not fitting in with the increasingly narrow definition of what it is to be normal in a highly structured regime. 'Asperger's' has become a by-word for coercing children towards an agreed political standard of normality, allegedly 'for their own good'. The assumption is that children are products and a product, as we all know, has to meet certain standards and criteria before it can be acceptable.

Children who are labelled are often also involved in bullying - sometimes as the hyperactive inflictors of rage, though more often as the victims - for which they are often perceived as dysfunctional. The weight of expectations about what someone must look and behave like in order to fit in is then added to this already distressing scenario. In an ethos where the product mentality is operating, a child who waits until everyone has got started on the work the group has been instructed to do, before asking, *"And what should I do?"* attracts a host of 'faulty product' labels. Options are worked through. Should the child be seen as 'deaf'? Should the child be seen as 'deliberately annoying' and brought up to specification with behavioural modification? Should the child be seen as 'slow', an apparently useful label when another of his responses to instructions is sometimes to follow them literally. It does not take much imagination to conjure up the reactions the parents would receive when a child who is told to undress for P.E. does just that. Teacher product requirements are that children should be compliant and, at least to some extent, bright. School ground product requirements may vary from school to school, but it is not uncommon that a boy of six, for example, should be expected to be tough, have good ball skills and not wear glasses.

Faced with the prospect that their child is becoming seen as a stupid or weak product, parents - far from questioning the fundamental assumption that children are products at all - will often go to great lengths to find other attributes that counter the faulty-product perception. The child is now further objectified, not with labels like 'stupid', 'clumsy'; but with others like 'highly articulate', 'idiosyncratic'. Caught up in the product mentality and desperate to prove their child's worth, parents can easily compile their own list of labels or characteristics which, on good days, function as cute eccentricities of which to be fond; and, on bad days, become an embarrassment, a signal of their own parental failure to produce the longed-for masterpiece. Faced with such a burden of angst and guilt, it is unsurprising that many parents are relieved when a scientific sounding, diagnostic label comes along to alleviate their worst fears - that they have caused their child to be a faulty product.

Under the protection of 'diagnosis', the list takes on the authority of not being merely a group of commonplace and wrongly attributed labels that could be used to diminish the humanity of thousands of other children who display their individuality, but rather an explanatory framework for the child's inability to function within the demands of the institution. This does not give rational credibility to such diagnoses. The world is full of children (and adults) who talk before others have finished their turn, who introduce non-sequiturs into conversation or who use language very literally. Many children have apparently quirky fears. Not everyone responds to social signals and eye gestures. Not everyone likes to be hugged. There are hosts of people who can amaze us with memories all the way back to babyhood, but still forget the last thing that was said to them. Many people never conquer spelling and handwriting, but still soak up factual knowledge or become totally engrossed in specific topics to the exclusion of all else. It is not rare to find able people who seem to have great co-ordination in an activity like playing the violin, but none-the-less wander around with untied shoe laces, seeming clumsy, awkward and ill at ease in their bodies.

The list of differences, many of them subtle, some of them slightly surreal, could go on. Having a unifying label for the set of characteristics that make up a parent's perceptions of one child at just one moment in time is no substitute for taking the child seriously as an autonomous individual in her own right. It is this which home-based education offers, particularly for those families that choose a non-coercive model of parenting and education. The *Taking Children Seriously* parenting philosophy states that it is possible to bring up children without coercion. Starting from the assumption of personal autonomy for everyone, even children, it sets out a theory for living consensually, positing that with sufficient openness, rationality and creativity, all parties in a relationship can reach common preferences. These are not compromises, but genuine win-win situations. Living without coercion is a radical undertaking for even the most formerly liberal of parents. Being fallible, the families that attempt it are far from perfect, but the serious undertaking to strive continually for no coercion has major ramifications for every way in which a family interacts. (cf Fortune-Wood, Jan, *Without Boundaries*)

The road of assessment, labelling and therapy is no doubt paved with the good intentions of those who want to help 'different' children to fit in for their own good, but it inevitably diminishes individuality and autonomy. *Taking Children Seriously* enables parents to begin questioning the usefulness of the label *per se*. This is an emotive area. Many parents find it an enormous relief to have a label that makes sense of all the differences they have been experiencing. For them, the label might function as a king of absolution; it enables them to believe that their child has an 'illness' that they did not cause. For others, it is a useful description, a short hand for a particular group who seem to share many similarities in behaviour or outlook. The label can also be seen as a highly effective way of gaining assistance. One person, for example, described the problems of Asperger's Syndrome as being similar to those of wheelchair users in their need for help:

> *"... there are some people who need special help. If someone can't walk it doesn't mean they need someone else to take charge of their lives, but it does mean they need a wheelchair, and some ramps around so they can go to places. Apsergers are like this, they are not different so that they need to be controlled, but they still have a disability which on occasions means they need something like a wheelchair."*

This sounds so reasonable, but is it? Many children are 'different' within the broad cultural terms that elevate certain characteristics and denigrate others, but what makes these cultural terms normative or right in the first place? Is having a tendency to become engrossed in particular subjects to the exclusion of other things objectively a bad thing, or is it merely that it doesn't fit with the school regime of dividing the day up into artificial subjects corralled into time allotments which are controlled by bells? Is a propensity to express extreme and (to others) seemingly bizarre anxieties a symptom of a recognisable disease or simply a child's response to various coercive stresses? Is Asperger's a pathology comparable to spinal paralysis or is it a convenient fiction which gives conventional parenting and education the justification for coercing highly individual children into conformity and narrow functionality?

If we lived in a society that truly tolerated difference and idiosyncrasy in all its human glory, then we would not feel a surge of relief on hearing that our child has been given a label, (which is actually some recognition of a child's individuality, but in a negative way in this context). If we lived in a society that took for granted the premise that all education should be centred in the individual and should be intrinsically motivated by the learner, rather than extrinsically motivated by government or parents, then the pursuit of 'assistance' for children who are currently diagnosed as having Asperger's would have no meaning. We do not live in such a society, but that in itself is not sufficient reason to succumb to poor thinking. Home education offers the possibility of children diagnosed as having Asperger's being brought up and educated solely on the basis of their own self-determined needs and interests, and not on the basis of a list of characteristics, which can never do justice to all that an individual is. Faced with diagnoses which seem to have scientific and medical currency, it can be easy for parents to succumb to labelling their child as a means of helping the child, little suspecting that what they are actually being offered is a system of control to suit the child to the context. As David Deutsch succinctly points out, what we actually have is a group of conventionally unwelcome characteristics, some of which are observed to greater or lesser degrees in a group of children who all resist mainstream conformity. *(see www.tcs.ac)*

Children are not products
Just thinking about our children in this demeaning way distorts the relationship and tends to exacerbate a whole range of subtle coercion. How is this so? One writer on the TCS list has developed the very useful image of the iceberg, something which is huge and constantly changing, and only fractionally visible.

> *"So I think of people as huge icebergs. When I look at my child and focus in on one aspect of him, I recognize that what I am seeing is not the 'whole' person by any stretch of the imagination. It is only the part of the iceberg that happens to be above water and visible right now, or that I happen to be focusing upon. I am then better able to be aware that my perception is far from accurate or the 'whole picture', it is only my interpretation of a small aspect of the person based on very very limited information - how can it be anything else when the bulk of that person is totally invisible to me?"*

The image of the iceberg is a helpful one in ridding ourselves of the tendency to seek labels for our children or to see them as, in any way, products of our parenting or education. It frees us from the need to construct our child as a perfect product, and allows us to realise that what we see of another person is simply what is visible at that time. It is a snapshot of a process, not a static definition.

If our children are not products, then what does it matter that at any one moment a child is consumed with a particular subject, that at another moment a child interrupts a conversation and that at another moment a child flinches away from touch? In a school environment it matters because an artificial environment with a determination to inflict a certain homogeneity of learning and behaviour is strongly in operation. This environment can be totally dispensed with in a home education setting where only the child's intrinsic motivation and autonomy govern what is learned. This does not mean that an autonomously educating parent would never communicate information about what others might expect in given situations, but this can be shared as suggestions and opinions with no compulsion on the child to comply and no judgments that define and objectify the child. The TCS writer adds:

> "Of course the knowledge that 'whatever is visible of the iceberg' is very much simply a matter of what I choose to see and how I choose to see it - that even looking at just what is above the surface is very 'non definite' - it is just my interpretation and is very subjective - is important too."

In a lifetime we are lucky if we come to understand ourselves well. Even if we do achieve this, we never really know the whole. It is presumptuous and demeaning to think that we can know another. We make observations, always partial, even if sometimes helpful. There is nothing wrong with offering up observations that might help our children; "If you don't look at people when you're talking you might find that they think you're lying.", "If you don't tie your shoe laces or ask someone to help you with them you might have an accident on your bike." This is reasonable and helpful, but it is not reasonable, helpful or necessary to coerce a child into making eye contact by placing him in some behavioural modification programme or by constantly barraging him with information that he has long since tired of hearing.

The point is to help the individual child live his own life by his own lights in the way that most pleases him, not to mould him into a new set of attributes which seem functional and pleasing to parents who want a higher level of product satisfaction, even when it is dressed up in the insidious cloak of being for the child's 'own good'. Once we have rid ourselves of the product mentality, the question of how we can help our children to become more functional, more acceptable, more socially in tune, more rounded individuals becomes not only irrelevant, but meaningless. The only question that remains is the same question that we should apply to all children, *"How can I as a parent help my child to do the things he wants with his life in ways that will not impose anyone's agenda but his own, in ways that will not seek to define or control or modify my child against his will?"* I am convinced that only through non-coercive interactions, only through home education that absolutely respects the child's autonomy, can we really be of assistance in our children's lives.

Children who are labelled with Asperger's Syndrome do not need more direction in their lives; they need considerably less. They need, primarily, to be freed from being seen as products or being objectified and defined by a list of subjective observations. They need parents, who are unquestioningly on their side, not to impose their own or so-called expert agendas on their children in the name of loving assistance, but simply to assist their children in carrying forward their own intrinsically motivated lives in process. To do this requires a willingness to ask radical questions and to let go of many entrenched assumptions about education, psychology and parenting, to name but a few. It requires going against mainstream and often allegedly expert opinion. It is not an easy path. It is not a neglectful path. It is a moral path that puts the individual above any of our partial perceptions and involves parents in constant engagement on the child's terms. It is possible.

(Material in this section, *Educating to the Label* revised from *Living Without the Label*, Fortune-Wood in *Paths are Made By Walking*, ed. Dowty and Cowlishaw)

A government-funded institution, which is full time and compulsory for anyone registered (currently 93% of school aged children), is going to serve policy first and not individuals. This is so, no matter how responsive the educational system attempts to be, and no matter what educational theory and practice is currently in vogue. Individual children who choose to use schools, supported by parents, and who attend school knowing that they can decide to deregister at any time, are a tiny minority for whom schools may work. For the rest, under compulsion and largely on their own in a monolithic system that demands conformity and a very specific style of functionality, school can be an enormously costly experience with potentially life-long repercussions. Home education explodes the myth that this constant sacrifice is mandatory. Home-based education allows individual children to flourish.

Chapter five

Resources not experts

Compulsory, free education has many costs; the country pays *en masse* for a system to which the 'beneficiaries' have never consented and which constantly escalates in price. Individual children pay with their welfare, privacy, emotional well-being and chances of becoming rational, creative, autonomous humans. In this chapter I will move on to examine the **skill** costs of free education. Within the education system, both parents and children are deskilled in favour of so called 'experts'. I propose that both philosophically and pragmatically, as we move into an event-driven, post-modern society, such de-skilling is an inappropriate outcome for education and must be replaced by a culture of mentors and resources.

A place for experts

There are many fields in which expertise is valuable and should be ignored only rarely and after serious consideration. In a diverse world, varied skills are increasingly important. It is extremely beneficial to human progress that we have a wide assortment of skills and passions across the human race. We do not all need to be medical experts, theoretical physicists, creative writers, or mechanics. It is a bonus of human creativity that we can rely on those who have skills and expertise different from our own to enrich our existence as we enrich theirs. There are arenas, however, where the proper role of experts and the interdependence that arises from it has been projected into wholly inappropriate areas, resulting not in those with skills enriching the general life, but rather disempowering many. Teaching, particularly as it is practiced in schools, is, I consider, one of these areas.

> *"Is it any wonder Socrates was outraged at the accusation that he took money to teach? Even then, philosophers saw clearly the inevitable direction the professionalization of teaching would take, pre-empting the teaching function that belongs to all in a healthy community; belongs, indeed, most clearly to yourself, since nobody else cares as much about your destiny. Professional teaching tends to another serious error. It makes*

> *things that are inherently easy to learn, like reading, writing,*
> *and arithmetic, difficult - by insisting they be taught by*
> *pedagogical procedures."*
>
> (Gatto, J.T. (1991) *The Six-Lesson Schoolteacher*)

Learning and the creation of new knowledge is something that
happens inside the learner by a process of conjecture and refutation.
Children are not just empty buckets to fill up with the right
knowledge in the right combination. The most progressive teaching
that takes place in school is still externally motivated by the teacher
acting on behalf of a national curriculum, not intrinsically motivated
by the learner. In this, it is always sub-optimal. More
fundamentally, it is likely to assume an inductivist view of learning,

> *"The inductivist or Lamarkian approach operates with the*
> *idea of instruction from without, or from the environment. But*
> *the critical or Darwinian approach only allows instruction*
> *from within - from within the structure itself.*
>
> *"In fact, I contend that there is no such thing as instruction*
> *from without the structure, or the passive reception of a flow of*
> *information which impresses itself on our sense organs. All*
> *observations are theory-impregnated. There is no pure,*
> *disinterested, theory-free observation...*
>
> *"We do not discover new facts or new effects by copying them,*
> *or by inferring them inductively from observation, or by any*
> *other method of instruction by the environment. We use,*
> *rather, the method of trial and the elimination of error. As*
> *Ernst Gombrich says, 'making comes before matching': the*
> *active production of a new trial structure comes before its*
> *exposure to eliminating tests."*
>
> (Popper, Karl, *The Myth of the Framework*, pp. 8-9)

The notion of generalised expertise in the field of teaching is a
school-based myth perpetrated by a system that has a vested interest
in making learning appear to be impossible without its aid. This is
simply not the case. In her book *Those Unschooled Minds: home-*
educated children grow up, Julie Webb gives a diverse range of
examples of young adults who have developed their own spheres of
competence without the aid of schools or expert teachers. This is the
case even in subjects that are traditionally noted for being 'difficult'
or requiring a systematic, taught approach.

> *"Edward Proctor gave an example of something that sparked*
> *his curiosity, describing a process which is direct*
> *contradiction of normal school methods but appears to have*

done the trick for his self-motivation: 'I found some books in the library on advanced mathematics...This gives you the impetus to go and do something about it,...I think if it had been organised step-by-step I might have been very bored.'"
(Webb, Julie, *Those Unschooled Minds*, p.14)

Having cited examples of how home-educated children accessed learning in a multiplicity of styles, the majority based on self-directed interests, Webb concludes:

"Home-educated children have much wider learning opportunities than are possible in school, and are able to get deeply involved in an activity because of the lack of artificial subject boundaries and time constraints."
(Webb, Julie, *Those Unschooled Minds*, p.14)

Webb's findings are in stark contrast to government rhetoric, where currently the well-known saying 'Those who can, do, and those who can't, teach' is being re-packaged in the slogan, 'Those who can, teach.'

"Teaching is like no other career."

...claims the website of the teacher training agency:

"It gives you the opportunity to influence young minds, to shape lives for the better. It will change your life too. You'll find it intellectually stimulating, creative and endlessly varied. Every day brings a fresh challenge...You'll have the opportunity to work alongside highly skilled and committed people and the chance to develop your own knowledge and skills.

"Teaching is the ultimate profession. Because, of course, without teaching there are no other professions."
(www.canteach.gov.uk)

This myth is not borne out by the growing experience of home educators, which is increasingly well documented by researchers such as Webb, Rothermel, Meighan and Thomas. There exist more and more young people who arrive at careers across the spectrum of human endeavour without schooling and without being taught in institutional settings. The government would have us believe that learning relies on expert teaching conducted in discrete institutions costing a generous slice of the national budget, as can be seen from the government site on standards for qualified teacher status:

"The National Standards set out the professional knowledge, understanding, skills and attributes necessary to enter the profession or to carry out effectively the key tasks for those in leadership roles in schools.

The main aims of the National Standards are to:

- *set out clear expectations for teachers at key points in the profession;*
- *help teachers at different points in the profession to plan and monitor their development, training and performance effectively, and to set clear, relevant objectives for improving their effectiveness;*
- *ensure that the focus at every point is on improving the achievement of pupils and the quality of their education;*
- *provide a basis for the professional recognition of teachers' expertise..."*

(www.canteach.gov.uk/info/standards/index.htm)

'How are they ever going to learn if we don't teach them?' is a question that has as many answers as there are learners. It is not a justification for a whole institutional edifice which mandates that on third Friday morning in year 3, term 2 it must be a particular text that has to be deconstructed or how to read the time that must now be learned *en masse*. Learning has always occurred everywhere and will continue to do so, despite any government's best efforts to plan centrally for human resources. It is false to assert that 'without teaching there are no other professions' in the sense of children **needing** to learn from those whose 'expertise' is not primarily as practitioners in a field, but in teaching *per se*.

Moreover, children, subjected to the school myth of expertise soon understand that it is not learning *per se* that is at the heart of their end of the activity, but rather achieving the correct appearance of learning. The most 'expert' teachers are those whose students achieve the highest grades or at least make the most progress in terms of 'value added' learning. The pursuit is not for new knowledge gained by conjecture and refutation, but for the right ticks in the right boxes. Writing in the Daily Pennsylvanian, one home-educated young person described the contrasting experiences of home education with the college pursuit of grades:

"...grades are the biggest single impediment to learning. Contrary to popular wisdom, grades do not motivate people to learn. They motivate people to get good grades...Grades have little usefulness in the adult world...Tests are supposed to

measure what you've learned...how well tests actually measure learning is another matter. How many of us have crammed, regurgitated and promptly moved on?"

(Bergson-Shilcock, Amanda, quoted in *Growing Without Schooling*, issue *129, p.15*)

De-skilling and dependency

"Teaching is the ultimate profession. Because, of course, without teaching there are no other professions."

(www.canteach.gov.uk)

This is an extremely costly myth. It is a financial cost in tax payments, but more insidiously and more disastrously, it has enormous costs in creativity, motivation and skills. Education, spoon-fed to children as though they were empty containers, in a compulsory environment burgeoning with the lessons of the hidden curriculum, does not increase knowledge but feeds the twin tragedies of de-skilling and dependency. Libertarian thinkers are most noted for their critiques of de-skilling and dependency in many arenas, but in the field of education, beyond broad assertions that compulsory state schooling is anathema, there appears to be little detailed thinking on the cost to children.

In his article, *The Case Against the Welfare State,* Nigel Ashford has argued that welfare is:

"...immoral, against freedom of choice, creates welfare dependency, is ineffective, is run in the interests of the producers, and is inefficient."

(Ashford, Nigel (1993) *Dismantling The Welfare State: Why and How*; Political Notes 86.occasional paper for Libertarian Alliance)

Although my argument here is not with the welfare state *per se*, Ashford's arguments are certainly applicable to compulsory education:

"It is immoral because it is coercive: it forcibly redistributes income from taxpayers to those who are believed to deserve it by politicians. Moral behaviour can only be based on free choice.... One cannot demonstrate 'caring' with other people's money.

"The universality principle means that the service is provided free for all regardless of need.

> *"...The original idea...was to aid people through difficult periods, and then they would return to independence. Instead the state has created a class that is permanently dependent on the state for all their major decisions. They have a lack of sense of control over their own lives...."*
> (Ashford, Nigel (1993) *Dismantling The Welfare State: Why and How,* Political Notes no. 86, occasional paper for Libertarian Alliance)

Such thinking echoes strongly the urge to provide education for 'children's own good', without recognizing that their individuality and intrinsic motivation will only suffer in the process. Many conventional educationalists aim at providing a package that will lead to autonomy and flexible thinking. The irony is that the package itself militates against such developments for many people. Where autonomy and flexible thinking survive, it is more in spite of than because of a compulsory national curriculum. Ashford goes on:

> *"The negative unintended consequences of government actions, here as elsewhere, are nearly always greater than the positive intended ones, as in the old saying 'the road to hell is paved with good intentions'....the expansion of state education led to mass illiteracy, with the middle and upper classes as the primary beneficiaries of higher education...The gap between the goals and the outputs is immense.*

> *"The consumer has no choice of supplier, and in a monopoly situation the service is provided in the interests of the producer...*

> *"The benefits that are provided (some children are educated...) are at an excessive cost...Think what other benefits could have been achieved if those resources had been spent wisely by those in the best position to know their own interests."*
> (Ashford, Nigel (1993) *Dismantling The Welfare State: Why and How,* Political Notes no. 86, occasional paper for Libertarian Alliance)

We cannot seriously expect that if we tell our children where to spend most of their time, what to do, when to eat, when to go to the toilet, what to learn and how to learn it for eleven years of their lives, we will one day wake up to perfect products who combine autonomy and conformity, creativity and conventionality, flexibility and traditional values. Rather, we will find that in some large measure we have created people who think inside the box, who are dependent and lacking in self-motivation, or people who are in a constant state of rebellion and anger. This cannot be good for individuals, and neither can it be good for society.

Home education as the model of post-modern learning

On a recent Radio Four broadcast, a government spokesperson complained that the education system as we currently know it seems to be lacking in some ingredient that produces entrepreneurial spirit and flexibility. Not only is the 'input in, product out' conception of education philosophically flawed, but also it is pragmatically failing.

Despite this, the government and conventional educational thinking persist in believing that if we just tinker sufficiently with the inputs then the magical outcome will arise. Human beings are not writable CD-Roms. This conception is seriously mistaken. Flexibility cannot be achieved by central planning for children. It is an issue of trust, creativity and risk. It is a spin-off of treating children, not as future products, but as present autonomous human beings in their own right. Only the educational philosophy of *Taking Children Seriously* does this. TCS is not about working towards agendas, outcomes and products, but about treating children with moral dignity as autonomous individuals. It has a basic optimism that creativity, rationality, new knowledge and flexibility will be the by-products of such treatment.

Discussing the balancing act between parental rights, children's rights and the role of the state in educational provision, the United Nations Special Rapporteur has commented on the right to education that:

> *"The knowledge, skills and values that the generation of future adults will need in their lifetime is not only unknown but unknowable."*

(paragraph 72. Katarina Tomasevski, United Nations Special Rapporteur on the right to education, submitted in accordance with the Commission on Human Rights Resolution 1998/33)

Tomasevski also goes some way towards questioning the product mentality of conventional, compulsory education:

> *"The Special Rapporteur has consistently held that the notion of human capital questions the inherent worth of each human being which underpins human rights, as well as undermining the role of education in the promotion and protection of human rights. She feels that an appropriate human rights response to the notion of human capital ought to be forged, lest the*

underlying idea of the market value of human capital risks turning upside-down the idea that the economy should serve people rather than the other way around. The human-capital approach moulds education solely towards economically relevant knowledge, skills and competence, to the detriment of human rights values. Education should prepare learners for parenthood or political participation, enhance social cohesion and tolerance. A productivist view of education depletes it of much of its purpose and substance."

(paragraph 67. Katarina Tomasevski, United Nations Special Rapporteur on the right to education, submitted in accordance with the Commission on Human Rights Resolution 1998/33)

Taking Children Seriously takes this stance further, proposing that we can have no fixed agenda for what future adults will need, but assuming that children who are taken seriously today and who learn that they can meet their preferences in life now will go on rationally and creatively making the optimal decisions for their own lives with beneficial spin-offs. This is a risk-laden stance and assumes that self-interest is a good and moral basis for educational progress.

"...but will they be pleasant people? Are they not more likely to be spoilt brats who grow up into selfish, petulant adults?

"Such questions arise from a number of misunderstandings of self-interest. Firstly, why do we need to oppose self-interest and altruism? We are sadly used to the idea that if we are enjoying something it must be at someone else's expense, whereas if we are suffering we are helping someone else. Is this really the case? As a parent, I can derive huge satisfaction and pleasure from helping my child get what he wants. It is something I prefer to do. I am at once pursuing my own and my child's interest. As a worker, I can derive enormous satisfaction from my job, or I can choose to do it to support the people I love or to benefit the community. These goals do not need to be mutually exclusive. I am doing what I prefer on one or many levels and others benefit. Similarly, a scientist can pursue her passion and make discoveries that are of enormous benefit to humanity, or a researcher can follow his passion and create new knowledge of enormous consequence to many lives. It is when we are following our intrinsic motivation that we are both at our most self-interested and most creative, and likely to benefit others in a multiplicity of ways.

"Secondly, these questions wrongly assume that we can get inside the minds of others, particularly our children, and label their motivations. Why should a child who wants what he wants be called a 'brat'? What is it that makes us resent his clarity and self-knowledge and sense of self-worth?...Having children who can clearly state their initial preferences is a bonus in the process of finding common preferences, not a threat to our own autonomy.

"When children experience for themselves relationships of consent in which the needs of others can be taken seriously without infringing their own needs and wants, then they have no reason to fear the needs of others....Being 'self-centred' or 'pleasing ourselves' does not have to stand in opposition to finding common preferences and benefiting others with our creativity. This is a false and pernicious dichotomy that taking our children seriously can overcome."

(Fortune-Wood, J.,*Without Boundaries*, pp.87-88)

It is an unpredictable route to take, redolent of the Spanish proverb, 'Traveller, there are no paths, paths are made by walking.' It is a stance that explodes the myth that we can treat human beings, particularly children, as though they are inert factors in a centrally planned economy. The government is already seeing that the inputs they put in do not necessarily result in the desired outcomes. It is a terrifying thing to trust human nature, especially when we are so monumentally unaccustomed to trusting it in children. It is, however, the only moral and realistic thing to do and places the *Taking Children Seriously* philosophy at the cutting edge of post-modern progress.

The very fact of society's transitions to post-modern, event-driven living and work calls into question the role of compulsory mass schooling. As Mike Fortune-Wood has discussed:

"There are those who suggest we are in the throws of a social change as fundamental as the industrialisation of the 19th century and are now moving away from an industrial to a post-industrial economy....

"Industrial society is characterised by large-scale manufacture centred upon factories employing large numbers of workers who, due to restricted access to transport, live and play in close proximity to their place of work and each other. Such communities possess a high degree of homogeneity in behaviour and belief. The work on offer requires a moderate

level of education and that, therefore, is what is provided for the mass of the population. Individuals who deviate very far from a variety of norms are ejected from the community, perhaps by a shift in their class status or straightforward ostracism.

"Post-industrial society is characterised by much smaller units of production. Often requiring a high level of technical education....Work becomes fragmented and less hierarchical. ... Individuals relate more to a matrix of like-minded individuals scattered throughout a large geographical area...For the first time in human history, community ceases to be centred upon a geographical location ultimately expanding to the virtual communities of the world wide web ...

"Individuals are no longer tied to belief systems regulated by homogeneity of life experience. Rather, post-industrial society is characterised by an explosion of new beliefs and attitudes to go along with the explosion of new or different experiences and opportunities and a breakdown in the restrictions placed upon individual thought and expression. The concept of multiculturalism could extend to include not only those of differing ethnic backgrounds but those of the same ethnicity whose world views are so radically different as to describe them as being culturally divergent.

"Not all of society participates in the change but only a significant proportion in the same way that Britain still has large rural areas and can yet be classed as industrialised (in fact the definition adopted by most economists is more than 50% of the population as living in cities). The process is anything but complete. But in the same way that 10% of anything is a market, 10% of a population is a movement. When that 10% are no longer isolated individuals thinking the unthinkable, but part of a large minority who have the power to communicate, they expect the right of expression and the freedom to follow their chosen life style. "

Mike Fortune-Wood goes on to question the effect such a transformation might have upon education. The education debate of the mid-19th century aimed to keep young people off the streets, and to free their parents to work in factories and preventing them falling into immoral practices. Therefore, the very structure of schools reflected life in a factory - large classes, a rigorous code of discipline and strict hierarchical structure. School was a microcosm of society and a foretaste of the future for its inmates. The 1944 Education Act created Grammar, Technical and Secondary schools whose intakes were intended to be roughly proportional to industry's needs at the time. Later still, Callaghan's white heat of technology debate again aligned education with industry:

"This has reached its final expression with the department of education being joined with the department of employment...

"A large part of educational effort still has nothing to do with the overt curriculum, but rather with the hidden curriculum; the socialisation of the young and the teaching of those mores and attitudes which give society its cultural identity. But what identity can a post-industrial society posses? How does a school teach social attitudes and mores (other than the very basic like, 'murder is bad') in a society where few people agree upon anything? Divergence rather than homogeneity is the theme of the day.

"What is the likely reaction of parents faced with schools teaching attitudes etc. with which they can no longer identify? It seems to me that traditional mass education aimed at creating a more or less homogenous society will be rejected by more and more parents as they feel themselves more and more at odds with the values of the education system....

"Even those parents who would subscribe to traditional moral values will have difficulties within the mass education system since schools themselves will drop the most traditional policies in favour of more 'relevant' attitudes. Examples that come to mind are the difficulties some Christian parents now have with the style of religious education and the concerns felt by those parents who are concerned about discipline and the rejection of corporal punishment by schools. Disaffection will therefore come from both (or rather all) ends of the political spectrum."

Mike Fortune-Wood notes that the Government of the day will need to make some hard and radical decisions. The education system faces both the social tensions of a transforming society and also a rapidly changing technological base. Neither schools, nor large-scale industry, can keep pace with this change:

"Perhaps the Open University and Open College systems may be used as a model and of course the Internet is fast becoming an important tool in education e.g. distance learning. Already, as we know, a large minority of parents and children are opting for home-based alternatives to schooling, in addition to which schools are abandoning ever-growing numbers of

children as 'unteachable'. The exclusion rate is growing so fast that even the government is beginning to recognise it as a crisis and despite the exclusions many schools are being labelled as disrupted and failing.

"Education has always been a microcosm of society and the problems of today's education system reflects the fragmentation of belief within society. Whatever the future of education I believe we will live to see the end of the use of schools comprising traditional classes for mass education which in Britain has had a history of a mere 150 years in any form and only 50 years or so in its current form."

(Mike Fortune-Wood, first published in *Education Otherwise* newsletter)

In such conditions, the United Nations Special Reporter's insistence that we cannot know what the needs of the next generation may be with any predictable accuracy beyond the most general statements, is particularly timely. We are thrown back again onto trusting that self-interest and intrinsic motivation will, after all, result in lives of learning. Home educating families facilitate this intrinsic motivation in a variety of ways, amongst them by looking to experts who are practitioners in the field of interest.

Sharing a passion
Outside of schools, and released from its pale imitation of expertise, there are arenas where accessing the expert knowledge of others is a valuable component of self-motivated learning. Many home-educated children have found that mentors, or those who will work with them as apprentices, have greatly aided their ability to make conjectures and refutations in a field of interest, as Julie Webb notes:

"Nearly all the families appreciated the many advantages of working with appropriate and stimulating mentors out-side the home who suited a particular individual's learning style, and found ways for their children to achieve this. Sometimes other family members with particular interests were drafted in, ...more often adults with a particular skill, such as Harriet's puppeteer colleague were pleased to pass it on to a fellow enthusiast."

(Webb, Julie, *Those Unschooled Minds*, p.30)

Learning demands that we make conjectures and go through our own process of trial and error. Learning is an internal process, but this does not mean that we cannot benefit from others who are willing to share their theories and explorations with us. We do not each have to invent the wheel for ourselves. The question is not so much, 'Why should we ever listen to experts?' as it is, 'Why go to a teacher when there are real practitioners?' People who are passionate about their area of expertise often have no problem sharing that passion.

One home educating parent I know recently approached a university lecturer in botany to ask if her nine-year-old son could talk to him about his own interest in botany. She made the approach in some trepidation, expecting the lecturer to be too busy, especially to meet with a 'mere' nine-year-old, but the lecturer was delighted to oblige. Not everyone will say 'yes'. Some practitioners may be genuinely too busy or simply not interested in communicating in this way, but home-educated children are increasingly finding that others with skills and knowledge can be a wonderful resource, whether as paid helpers or as part of some barter of other skills and time from the child or her family or on a purely informal basis for the pleasure of sharing a passion.

This was certainly the experience of Julia Bergson-Shilcock, who, at 14 was looking for a non-traditional approach to science and veterinary studies. She began by simply attending weekday clinics at her local vet's surgery in order to observe.

> *"... the vet had so much patience and really wanted to explain things to me. As the weeks went on he started letting me do small parts of the job. Each week he gave me more and more responsibility. ...I continued to observe and help out weekly... Then my schedule started to fill up ...and I guess I had gone as far as I wanted to go with it at that point."*
> (Bergson-Shilcock, Julia, 'Observing Veterinary Surgery; Breeding Cats', *Growing Without Schooling*, issue *131, p.5)*

Alongside this experience, Julia began breeding cats, avidly taking an interest in the science that went alongside it, while also building up a business and the skills that went with marketing and accounting. By the age of 18, Julia was running a thriving business with a high reputation,

> *"One thing that made me feel great was when, after a few years, my old cat breeder I'd gone to when I was little 13-year-old started recommending customers to me."*
> (Bergson-Shilcock Julia, 'Observing Veterinary Surgery; Breeding Cats', *Growing Without Schooling*, issue, *131, p.5)*

This ability to access the passions of others and to share them has been written about most extensively by David Albert in his book, *And the Skylark Sings with Me*. In *Growing Without Schooling*, Albert writes:

> *"The constant challenge for us and for our children lay...in finding new ways to access our community, its people, and its resources...When utilizing the community as flexible learning environment...the whole point is to find individuals prepared and willing to share their deepest passions and most highly developed expertise...*

> *"...Instead of encountering teachers teaching A. and M. have had serious and sometimes lasting encounters and relationships with scientists and wildlife biologists undertaking research, musicians composing and performing, theater directors directing, poets writing, astronomers observing..."*
>
> (Albert, David, 'And the Skylark Sings with Me', *Growing Without Schooling*, issue 130, p.23.)

Sharing others' passions demands a lot of creative and flexible thinking. It demands that we creatively and constantly evolve ways to fulfill intrinsic motivation rather than merely relying on some pre-ordained package to spatter our children with information that may, or more likely, may not prove relevant.

> *"It has demanded constantly expanding our network of friends and acquaintances and carefully evaluating each new learning relationship... It has meant time regularly pursuing newspaper and community publications and calendars for potential opportunities, and a willingness to call strangers on the telephone and ask questions which may reveal either our partial or total ignorance. It has dictated an enormous amount of schedule juggling, and an ongoing day-to-day, month-to-month, year-to-year re-evaluation of the optimal relationship between our children's organized and unorganised activities... As we did so, we had to admit humbly to ourselves that each new solution we found was only tentative... We try to keep ourselves open, as we watch and listen."*
>
> (Albert, David, 'And the Skylark Sings with Me', *Growing Without Schooling*, issue 130, p.23.)

Playing the chance card
It also has to be recognised that in this event-driven, intrinsically motivated style of education there will always be an element of chance. Interviewing grown up home-educated young people, Julie Webb described this as the role of 'serendipity'.

> *"The importance of serendipity, and the lateral thinking that goes with it, crops up here again, together with being out and about enough in the real world enough to spot where the opportunities lie."*
>
> (Webb, Julie, *Those Unschooled Minds*, p.62)

Chance or serendipity are beautifully illustrated in David Deutsch's story of how one child might learn following her intrinsic motivation:

> *"Well OK, if you really insist on knowing, I'll tell you. I know all the details except her name, so let's call her Anna.*
>
> *"Sometime this year, Anna's previous interest in Lego, treehouse-building, the internet and computer games will all come together and draw her attention to a major TV documentary about how stunts are arranged in movies. She will start building such stunts in the garden, each more ingenious than the last, using all sorts of props and filming them on a video camera. One day, a physics teacher will walk past and see her doing this. Calling to her to give her advice about how to balance a particular arrangement of planks, he will inadvertently cause her to fall fifteen feet onto the grass, fortunately causing only a broken toe.*
>
> *"Anna will have to wait three hours for treatment in the emergency room, which could have been excruciating (because the slightly addled person waiting on her left suffering from chronic whiteboard-marker poisoning will be a mathematics teacher eager to plug the gaps in her home education) but in the event, it will pass quickly because she will get into conversation with the fascinating person waiting on her right, a huge lady called Agnes. Turns out Agnes' ex-husband used to do stunts in Hollywood and she used to help him before she found out about some of the other stunts he pulled -- but that's another story. Anyway, now she owns three successful cafes in town and has just bought two more and wants to go up-market. She's been talking to an advertising agency about making a series of ads for the local TV. She hasn't liked any of their ideas so far, but soon finds that Anna is bubbling with great ideas for how to advertise high-class restaurants using movie-like stunts. Agnes will be surprised and delighted to hear that Anna actually has videos of several stunts she has arranged single-handed (with a little help from her little brothers) and will tell her to drop by at her office next day.*

"Next day Anna will hobble along to Agnes' office above one of her restaurants, currently being re-fitted with the new up-market decor. Agnes will love the videos, and will commission Anna to design five stunts for the new series of ads, and execute them for the TV people. Anna will earn three thousand dollars for this, but think no more about it until six months later when the advertising agency will offer her a similar job, albeit for only $500. She will accept, because even though it's a lot of work and the materials alone will cost almost that much, she will enjoy it enormously. The following week, someone will let the agency down and they will phone around in desperation for anyone they know who can do a firework display.

"Anna will never have done such a thing, and technically it's illegal, but she will agree to step in to help them out. Not only will the display be a great success, but Anna will meet and fall instantly in love with...the computerised timing device that the agency gave her to time the fireworks. She will ask if she can borrow it, and for the next year it will spend far more time in her garage than at the agency, for she will think of more and more ways to use it to do wonderful stunts, and also special effects. She will also start editing her movies on the agency's professional computerised editing system.

"One day in the cutting room, she will meet a pro who is engaged in a science documentary. He will be a mathematics graduate - who has forgotten all the maths he ever knew and will now be spending all his time filming animals mating. So they won't talk about maths but she will show him how to hide some of the more repulsive aspects of his footage using a difficult timed transition on the editing machine, and in return he will introduce her to his boss, whose next documentary will be about the NASA robots that will one day explore Mars. Anna will be hired as a technical assistant on that documentary, and will dazzle everyone with the exciting stunts she will think of to demonstrate how these robots will behave on Mars. The boss will offer her a permanent job on the team, but she will refuse, because while at NASA, she will also have helped one of the astronomers out with making a promotional movie designed to persuade the government to fund more infra-red satellites. The problem will have been how to display, in an eye-catching and persuasive way, the complex data that demonstrate why such satellites are better than ground-based telescopes. Anna will succeed at this so well that she will have persuaded herself too. She will spend the next two years

working for one of NASA's subcontractors, first in the publicity department, then designing user-interfaces for satellite ground stations, and then even some aspects of the satellites themselves.

"All this will involve a lot of interactions between herself and astrophysics graduate students, but slowly the attraction of satellites will wear off, and she will realise that her real love is 'theoretical' astronomy. She'll read a book about calculus, do a six-month adult-education course in physics to fill in the gaps in what she's picked up, and then apply to take an undergraduate degree in astronomy, complete it a year ahead of time and then be accepted for a PhD in quasar structure. At that point she will officially become a SCIENTIST.

"Meanwhile she will have had two children with the NASA astronomer (who will have left astronomy to become an internet millionaire and failed miserably, but will by that time be blissfully happy again as a home maker) and she will worry that the children won't achieve anything in life unless they have a good grounding in the basics, especially mathematics, but for some unaccountable reason the ungrateful little wretches will be digging their heels in and refusing to listen."

(Deutsch, David TCS internet mailing list)

Experts have their place in education, particularly as mentors and resources for those setting out to make their own conjectures. Schools as they are currently constituted do not provide this kind of expertise. Rather, they fuel the myth that learning is an institutionalised activity separated from life, neatly packaged into artificial subject boundaries and delivered by those whose expertise is in 'teaching' *per se*. It is an exercise in control, conformity and mistrust and does not succeed even in what it sets out to achieve. Home education provides a valuable corrective to such conventional educational thinking; it is based on autonomy, on treating the child seriously as a moral agent with free will, capable of rational thinking. Home education, when it is centered on intrinsic motivation, makes the most of self-interest and is effective and optimal in its pursuit of relevant new knowledge. As we will explore in the final chapter, home education is the positive alternative to costly compulsory state schooling.

Chapter six

A positive alternative

In this concluding chapter I will argue that for autonomy and true freedom in education to flourish we need to look to the 'Do-It-Yourself' approach of home-based education, whether undertaken by individual families or by voluntary communities. Home-based education is a positive alternative to paying the costs of 'free' state provision. There are now many parents searching for alternative educational provision for their children. Some come to the decision fresh, with a young child who has not yet encountered any educational system. Many more are searching urgently for an educational model that will not go on compounding the damage that the child has already sustained, and will enable the child to rediscover his/her own sense of intrinsic motivation and self esteem.

The sad reality is that many parents come to home-based education as a negative response to what is on offer within mainstream or special needs schooling. Sometimes it may even be seen as a last resort or an unwelcome necessity. This is the time to revise that opinion. No matter what the motivation for investigating or choosing home-based education, home education can always be a positive choice. It is a viable and discrete educational alternative, not merely a reactionary expedient for those who feel they have run out of options (even if that is where some parents and children are starting from.)

Accentuating the positive
All parents play the role of educator in the child's first years when the growth and learning is more rapid and comprehensive than any that subsequently takes place. The expanding role of schools, not just in delivering basic education, but also in assuming control over social and welfare functions, has increasingly de-skilled and disempowered parents. The primary responsibility for a child's education rests, in law, with the parents. The majority of people choose to delegate that responsibility to schools. Home educators are those who choose not to delegate the responsibility, but to take that primary responsibility for themselves. Moreover, they do so

for a growing number of positive reasons, amongst which are:

- Meeting a child's educational needs according to his or her age, ability and aptitude and any special needs can be individually dovetailed to the specific child, making home education pre-eminently efficient.
- The learning environment can be precisely tailored to individual learning styles and multiple intelligences. The environment is friendly to the learner without any unwanted distractions of procedure or administration and the conditions can be precisely fitted to the person. Thus, one child might prefer to work in a stimulating environment, full of sound and colour, while another chooses a calm, quiet environment.
- The friendly learning environment focuses on strengths and builds self-confidence and self-esteem. Criticism comes only as something constructive and welcome.
- The child, together with his or her family, defines and creates the environment rather than the environment defining, and labelling, the child.
- Home education must be full time, but there is no stipulation over exact hours or days, enabling families to work, learn, live and play with maximum flexibility. Families practising home-based education are free to pursue event-driven lifestyles rather than clock-driven lifestyles, giving them maximum flexibility and access to an increasingly event-driven society.
- We now live in an information rich world and with growing access to a wide range of media including television, video, music, radio, CD-Roms and Internet. It is both possible and desirable for parents and children to work together to foster personalised learning.
- The notion of a government-controlled curriculum is replaced with the more positive notion of learning which is specifically responsive to the intrinsic motivation of the child and/or the educational philosophy of the family.
- Home education gives children access to developing research skills in which they increasingly learn to control and manage their own learning. This equips them to be real researchers and producers of knowledge, not just consumers of pre-defined educational packages.
- Home education promotes a sense of being in control and responsible, with children not only being partners or the leading protagonists in their own education, but also in charge of simple human functions (such as getting snacks or drinks or going to the toilet) thus promoting confidence and maturity.

- Education becomes part of a wider vision of developing and supporting moral and humane family and societal institutions.
- Children remain a full part of local communities, with the ability fully to access community facilities, such as libraries, shops, museums, exhibitions, theatres, transport, art centres on a full time basis.
- Learning is responsive and integral to the whole family lifestyle and ideology, whether the model is one of respecting children's autonomy, developing a family style of democracy or adhering to a particular religion or ideology.
- Parents remain integral to their children's learning and development, maintaining key roles such as trusted advisor, coach or teacher.
- Social skills can be developed within the community across a full range of age groups.
- There is more time available for discovering and optimizing special interests and skills.
- Areas of learning can be studied and followed up to exactly the depth required in each instance. There is no compulsion to either cut short study because of the demands of a generalized curriculum, nor to pursue subjects beyond the point of interest and value to the individual.
- Learning is focused on wanted and needed information.
- In the familiar and small scale environment of the home, supplemented by access to the community and its facilities, home-educated children are able to employ what Roland Meighan has called 'purposive conversation' as their primary learning tool, to great effect.

There are many negative reasons why people might initially find themselves wondering if home-based education is the only route left open to them, particularly with children whose individuality is less amenable to institutional demands and who have suffered as a result. There is no need to remain with these negative motivators. Home-based education is a positive choice, not least of all because it is the only educational alternative that can be absolutely responsive to the individual child. Such individual responsiveness comes as a welcome relief for families who feel that their child has already sustained damage from the educational system, however well meaning, whilst others feel fortunate to have had access to home education from the beginning.

A singular education

Any educational system that envisages working with groups of children must, by its nature, be aimed at some imaginary typical child. It is remarkable that any children manage to comply with this level of standaristion; few remain completely undamaged by the demands of compulsory institutional conformity; and for many children, such demands are, not unreasonably, intolerable. The response of the educational machine to these children is not to change and adapt the system in order to take account of each child's individuality and intrinsic learning motivation. That is not how institutional structures work, even if the individuals within them have good intentions. All too often children, and sometimes their whole families, find that the problem of large institutions (being unsuited to making humane, small-scale individual responses) is redefined as a problem of individual child or family dysfunction.

With home-based education, there is no one educational system to slot into. The child and parents mould the learning. The learning does not mould the child. This distinctive sort of education sets home-based education apart from any other learning system. This singularity also makes for a wide diversity of educational styles, methods and philosophies between home educators, so that 'home education' becomes a vast umbrella term for an endlessly innovative variety of educational provisions.

The spectrum of home education covers every approach and educational school of thought, from the most structured and formal to the most autonomous and radical, but whatever the operative paradigm it will never look like a school. Even where work is set, texts books are used, finished work is dated and kept, set hours are adhered to and specific learning outcomes are planned for and evaluated, home education remains significantly distinctive. This is because there is still a degree of interaction, level of purposive conversation, use of community facilities, wider accessing of information resources, individualized learning environment and the ability to be responsive to the particular skills and interests of the child, that can never be imitated by an institutional setting.

Most parents come to home education with school as the dominant model of what education looks like, but in fact schooling need have no bearing on our concept of education. Many home educators, even when they start with a high degree of structure, gradually discover the benefits of flexibility in varying measures. Some opt for a totally non-coercive paradigm of parenting and education in which the lines of demarcation between living and learning become increasingly hard to define. Whatever the model, many home educators find that no two days look the same and that, increasingly, exploring the world and purposive conversation become primary methods of learning.

From theory to practice

The question for those considering home-based education is not 'why?', but 'why not?' After all, parents have the primary responsibility for children's education. It is a relatively recent phenomenon that parents *en masse* hand their children over to the state without question for increasingly longer periods of their childhood, at younger and younger ages.

Many parents are already highly aware of the negative effects of school on their children. Many fear that a child who has not yet gone to school will at worst be traumatised and labelled, or at best be repressed by the demands of the educational system. Faced with such fears and reality, home education can present itself as a positive alternative, not least of all for the over-riding advantage of facilitating an individualised, singular educational environment for each child. The choices are legion and the educational style and philosophy of each family can be unique. There is no blueprint, but a growing wealth of theory, experience, information and support to draw on, much of it from home educators themselves who have an increasing diversity of networks and publications to support those just beginning. Home-based education means something different to each family; the consistent thread is the flexibility to develop a learning environment that is personalised and responsive to the individual. Some families feel strongly that an imposed structure must prevail, others prefer a mixture of imposed structure and child-led learning, whilst others follow an autonomous philosophy, advocating that only intrinsically motivated learning is true education. Whatever route families take, they find that the style evolves over a period of time. Certainly, home-based education can give everyone a unique and positive way to forge alternative environments of individualized learning. Most especially, home-based education allows families to:

- retain philosophical control and personal accountability
- preserve choice over the content of education
- build an educational culture which respects civil liberties and the needs of individual children
- promote divergence, individuality and emotional health amongst their children

- focus the skills base in families, with the culture of experts transformed into a culture of resources.
- model a system that leads the way in event-driven, flexible, modern living and learning.

Philosophical control

Educational philosophy is not a homogenous body of knowledge that has been universally agreed upon. For some, the words 'education' and 'school' are all but synonymous; for others, 'education' is a part of a fluid learning that takes place within life and which demands intrinsic motivation. Others question the use of the word 'education', pointing out that even discourse about what is 'educational' or not impedes the growth of knowledge that simply takes place when individuals are able to meet their own preferences.

Aside from those very few children who make a positive decision to attend school for their own purposes, school allows no control of educational philosophy. The cost of this 'free' resource is that parents and children **must** subscribe to the whole package of whatever is on offer. What counts as education is laid down through a complex mixture of government policy, national curriculum, school ethos and the expectations and style of the individual teacher. Parental responsibility is reduced to ensuring that the child attends at all times (barring periods of illness which can be properly accounted for) and co-operates fully with the dictates of the school. 'Good' parents are those who support what the school aims to achieve in terms of learning and conformity, not those who have a stance on the philosophy of education or who support their child in having her own stance on the nature of education.

The benefits of having philosophical control within the family are enormous and far-reaching. For families whose whole philosophy of life is fundamentally at odds with the culture of schooling, this is particularly the case. It may be because of a particular religious outlook - for example, many Muslim or Christian families find that school does not suit the values they wish to communicate. Or, it may be because of alternative lifestyle choices, as Julie Webb indicates in *Those Unschooled Minds* (p.33) where parents 'downshift' to live more simply by doing work at home, supporting environmental campaigns or becoming self sufficient. It may be on philosophical grounds, such as wanting to retain control of education or wanting to support children's autonomy. All of these options are made possible by home-based education, allowing an enormous diversity of lifestyle and theory to develop and flourish.

This is supportive for any family who wants even a modicum of philosophical control, but it particularly supports those whose educational philosophies veer sharply from conventional thinking, such as those who support *Taking Children Seriously*. TCS does not view education as a package to be imbibed, but as a lifestyle of creativity and rationality, solving problems by a process of conjecture and refutation and thereby creating new knowledge. Children and adults attempt to live together without coercion in their relationships, through a process of reaching common preferences; that is, solutions that everyone genuinely prefers. Within such a philosophy, children's autonomy is supported and learning is intrinsically motivated.

> *"Autonomy is the right of self-government and free will. Education is the process by which we develop intellectual potential and foster the growth of knowledge. Education relies on a rational development of conjecture and refutation. Autonomous education is simply that process by which knowledge grows because of the intrinsic motivation of the individual. In fact, the core to understanding autonomous education is in understanding the absolutely fundamental and unshakeable role of intrinsic motivation. It is quite common to find autonomy juxtaposed with other educational concepts in order to attempt to denigrate and stereotype the theory. It is not uncommon to hear that an autonomously educated child is effectively considered to be barred from ever sitting an exam or gaining a qualification; from ever learning anything which involves specific teaching; from ever achieving certain kinds of academic knowledge etc. All of these suppositions are false. The one thing that is always inimical to learning in the sense that autonomous educators understand it is extrinsic motivation, i.e. coercion....*
>
> *"Intrinsic motivation requires the freedom of self government."*
>
> (Fortune-Wood, *Doing It Their Way*, pp.26-27)

This is not the kind of philosophy that can flourish in a compulsory state institution, but it is precisely the kind of philosophy that can lead to a life and learning that is integrated in a constant search for new knowledge.

Content and style
Not only does home-based education ensure that the philosophical framework of education is not simply handed over to the state; but it also guarantees that the content of education is not externally

ordained and there is no prescribed style of how children should learn. Myth has it (and it could be true) that there are home educating families who have desks in rows and children in uniforms working through curricula for set hours every day, with timetables and lunch breaks and terms and all the familiar paraphernalia of schools. It is certainly the case that a few home educators see schools as simply not doing enough of what they set out to do and who set out to compete, producing hot-housed children who achieve exam successes at young ages. It is not a route I could go down after years of exposure to the TCS philosophy, but it is certainly one that I understood and had a lot of sympathy for when I first began the adventure of home-based education. Latterly, I have come to realise that what we are seeking as a family is not simply 'more' and 'better' by conventional educational standards, but something totally different. Not everyone would agree or aspire to this difference, but what home education allows is that there is no such thing as a typical educational day or week.

Even within those who share a philosophy, the actual content and style of what is taking place might differ radically between families. It might be that two families happen to have a very structured, formal approach with high academic expectations placed on the children and yet between them look very dissimilar; with one family having a bias towards sciences and another towards arts and music, one family working in very discrete subject boxes and the other taking a more thematic approach. On the other hand, there may be two TCS families. The first could look, to the casual observer, every bit as structured as a 'formal' family because the child has **chosen** to do a specific range of exams for her own ends, whilst the second might look as though no 'education' (as it is commonly conceived) is taking place because the child is fulfilling his intrinsic motivation through television programmes, sketching and tree climbing. Even within one TCS family, because intrinsic motivation is paramount, there might be several styles of education and varied educational content over the course of one day, much of which might not be recognisable as education to those with a conventional mentality, with yet other parts that would be very recognisable and approved.

The benefit of such freedom over content and style is that whatever learning takes place can be optimal. People learn well if the learning is something they want and need for their own ends, if it makes sense to them within their own life and context. Home educating parents routinely report that children who have resisted learning to read or who have shown problems with literacy for years suddenly become fluent readers as soon as they have some text that it is important for them to be able to decipher and use for themselves. Similarly, whether the area is maths, science or spelling, home-educated children regularly find that they can acquire knowledge very quickly, even knowledge that their school peers have taken years to 'build up' to, when it is something they **want** to know.

Home-educated children have the benefit of not having to suffer from the myth of 'necessary knowledge', some amorphous body of knowledge that no-one can ever quite agree on, but which convention still insists **must** be learnt if the child's life is not to become a total disaster.

> *"Autonomous educators are confident that children will learn whatever children deem for themselves to be essential, whether it is the required body of knowledge to enter a medical career or the history of twentieth century film-making or how to build a tree house. In educational law there is no concept of attempting to cause a child to know any particular essentials, but rather of ensuring that education is 'efficient'...What could be more efficient than a child learning something to suit his or her own intrinsic and individual purposes?"*
> (Fortune-Wood, J., *Doing It Their Way*, p.49)

Education with liberty
Control of the philosophy of education and of its style and content are foundational to home education's contribution to civil liberty. The issue of whose liberty is at stake being moot; within home educating circles there is a wide spectrum of opinion as to whether the parents' liberty to choose the 'right' education for their own children outweighs the child's liberty to choose their own education. Only the TCS philosophy completely supports the child's primacy of autonomy (even when, controversially, this might occasionally entail a child choosing school as opposed to being forced into school). All home-based education options, however, offer some benefits in terms of liberty.

Just as schools may have an alarmingly narrow definition of 'education', they have a correspondingly alarming and all-encompassing notion of what areas of a child's life they should control in the name of this education. Dress, shoes, hair styles, even what bags can be carried, are routinely prescribed. Infringements upon such codes can result in detentions (encroachment into even more of the child's individual time) or temporary exclusions.

Ironically, children who do not 'look' the part are deemed unfit to receive the compulsory and otherwise 'essential' education. Language is another controlled area. A child who swears is apparently in no fit state to learn maths nor to read about Chaucer's 'shitten' shepherd or Shakespeare's 'base bastard'.

These constant attacks on liberty do not stop at the school gates. I recently heard one head teacher telling his pupils that he had asked local shopkeepers to inform on any 'bad' behaviour. He promised to institute whole school punishments, via detentions, if he received negative reports; a tactic no doubt designed to encourage inmates to inform on each other rather than risk being falsely implicated.

Such affronts on liberty are so endemic that most adults have ceased to notice them, and many children have become resigned to them or have found necessarily devious ways to survive them. The quality of this survival is sadly questionable, especially when the child is perceived as not conforming or not measuring up to the correct product specifications. In such circumstances, children are too frequently subjected to a barrage of psychotherapy or behavioural modification. This all too often becomes family therapy, with the child's nonconformity projected into some dubious family dysfunction. One home educating parent recently reported how, after taking one child out of school, her whole family had been subjected to spurious criticism and invasive scrutiny. This parent had enjoyed very cordial and supportive relationships with the school where her other children remained happy to attend and where none of her children had previously been seen as 'difficult', but after one child made the decision to learn at home, the others were accused of using bad language, of being difficult to control, of being left up late every night watching inappropriate TV programmes. All of these bogus accusations were said to be occurring because of the 'bad influence' of the home-educated child. Similar tales are legion. In some cases, the bad feeling and destructive comments go much further than undermining the parents' confidence.

This is certainly the contention of Vin Suprinovicz in his article, *Educrats Declare War on Remaining Parental Rights*. Suprinovicz cites a number of disturbing cases in which children are removed from their homes on very flimsy grounds, all related to state control of family life rather than to genuine child welfare, before going on:

"The presumption in America today - first for the poor but increasingly for all of us - is that our children belong to the state. The state allows those children to remain 'out on loan' to their natural birth parents only so long as you meet all the government's requirements...

"And you'd better make sure your kid reports to the local government youth propaganda camp from the age of six...or is it 5 now?...so the local educrats get their subsidies based on a full complement of little butts to warm the seats...or else.

"Now comes Senate Bill 73...The bill 'requires state board of education to prescribe forms for reports of parental involvement in education of children.'...

"The teachers union would help draft a form on which teachers would grade parents on 'whether the parent or legal guardian ensures the attendance and punctuality of the pupil, including, without limitation, whether the pupil: (1) Completes his homework assignments in a timely manner; (2) Is present in the classroom when school begins each day ...

"Also required would be...The parent and child abide by any applicable rules and policies of the school and the school district; and ... whether the parent or legal guardian: (1) Completes forms and other documents that are required by the school or school district in a timely manner; (2) Assists in carrying out a plan to improve the pupil's academic achievement, if applicable; (3) Attends conferences between the teacher and the parent or legal guardian, if applicable; and (4) Attends school activities.'

"This police state measure goes on to assure us that the new parental report cards shall not 'interfere unreasonably with the personal privacy of the parent and his child or the legal guardian and his ward.'...the trick being that educrats...will get to define the word 'unreasonably'"...

"The premise of public education is that these 'experts' with their fancy 'Ed' degrees know far more about what and how our kids should learn than do we 'uneducated' boobs. Yet they're now so desperate to shift the blame for their failures that they seek a way to document 'bad parental involvement' as the main culprit.

"Parental involvement? Taxpaying parents who show up with detailed instructions on the course of study and method of instruction best suited to their individual child - let alone

concerns or demands involving library books and sex education curricula - need not apply. Our only job...is to gratefully pay up, while teaching our children to obediently prostrate themselves before the altar of the almighty state.

"My advice?...Pull your kids out of the government schools, today."

(Vin Suprinovicz, *Educrats Declare War on Remaining Parental Rights,* Mountain Media: The Libertarian (2001)

It may well be true that there is a more liberal spirit abroad in Britain than in the land of the free, but the same problems exist, even if they tend to be more subtly expressed. If we delegate our responsibility for education to state institutions that, once the child is registered become compulsory until we deregister, then we give away not just some discrete and containable aspect of our child's life, but a much wider remit to interfere with family life and privacy. Home education has the potential to nullify such affronts on liberty. Though it is not a cast iron guarantee that children will be accorded the autonomy that is rightfully theirs, since it is at least theoretically possible that there are some homes where the regime is more oppressive than we might find in school, home education does create the opportunity for families to avoid the excesses of institutional conformity and, at best, it allows genuine respect for liberty.

Divergence
Outside of prescribed curricula and the agendas that accompany them, diversity can flourish. Diversity is a benefit not only to families (and to children where they are respected as having this control for themselves) but also to society. There is a common fear and misapprehension that by encouraging 'bowling alone' (a term coined to describe individualised education which is not conformist) home education will in some sense contribute to the downfall of society. This is simply not the case. Rather, home education is part of a postmodern pattern in which community is redefined not in terms of location or homogeneity, but in terms of interest groups. Writing on an alternative education forum Internet mailing list, Mike Fortune-Wood noted:

"The issue of privatisation of the family is one which has been noted in the UK...Home education is just an extension of this.

"...The rise in home education in the UK is caused by the growing confidences of the new middle classes and the rise in wealth of the working class accompanied by a fall in the trust

of social institutions. Home educators have decided that Schools have failed their children and that they are no longer willing to put up and shut up regarding the social control placed upon them and their children. I believe that this is going to be a growing movement as we become more post-modernist.

"As belief systems fracture and diverge we will experience less commonality in submission to all kinds of institution. They will be replaced by more interest group led movements. - Home education is just one of them.

"Almost every institution I have had contact with in my life has failed me, they have all expected me to fit them rather than they adapting to my needs...It's no longer to do with social capital - they could rebuild every school in the country and fund them like Eton with class sizes down to 3 and still we wouldn't send our kids.

"...community is no longer geographically based and this is the crux of the matter, anyone who 'goes to a place looking for a community' is not going to find it, he must look for interest groups - like Home education."

(Fortune-Wood, Mike, *Homeschooling Alone,* post to aerolist@edrev.org, *March 4th 2001)*

The diversity allowed by home education is of incalculable benefit for individuals. Conformity, on the other hand, is very costly to individuals; sometimes it entails humiliating labelling and treatment, and it often involves trauma, emotional harm and damage to rational thinking. The dark side of free, compulsory state provision of education is that, without any consultation or consent, children find themselves as the unwitting half of a contract mandating that they take up the provision with the responsibility to function within its narrow dictates. In any other walk of life, we would be appalled at such treatment of other human individuals. We have somehow convinced ourselves that children are not yet fully human, that their age prevents them from feeling these things too deeply, that their youth renders them malleable without much consequence.

This is not the case. It is an astonishing fact that many children who in school are diagnosed with syndromes such as ADHD or Asperger's syndrome have no noticeable 'disability' within months of leaving school to be home educated. How can home education cure what major drugs and therapy struggle to contain? It cannot.

The sad truth is that no cure was ever needed. Children need to be taken seriously as individuals. A difference in how one child's brain processes information or interprets faces (if such difference exists) is not a reason to demand conformity and medicate accordingly.

Home education celebrates diversity and individuality. Parents can become trusted advisors and helpers with a key role to play in giving their children information about what might be expected in certain contexts, about how people might view certain patterns of speech or interaction or dress. Parents can help children to guess possible consequences of actions and to take steps to ensure that any negative consequences are worked through or around. Children who might be viewed as 'problems' in school can feel the relief not of being solved, but of having their concerns addressed, their strengths supported and encouraged and criticism given as gifts to be used or not.

A culture of resources
The world is teeming with expertise and knowledge. We live in an information-rich age with increasingly cheap access to powerful learning tools. Assisted by parents who are on their children's side and willing to facilitate the growth of knowledge that their children desire, there is every possibility that home education can make optimum use of the wealth of resources available. No matter how innovative and committed individual teachers are, they begin with enormous impediments. They have very little time for any one individual and pursuing focused, purposeful conversations with any one child is a rare luxury. They have a pre-ordained agenda to work to and cannot digress into areas of interest. It is a moment of unusual luck when even one student really wants to be learning that particular thing on the curriculum on that particular day, at that particular time and by that particular method. Few, if any of the students, will be in the class by consent. Despite the enormous national budget that goes into education, they will always be struggling with the budgetary constraints of what is left over for actual classroom resources.

Home education begins from a much more positive base. Even in a large family, the opportunities for attentive, constructive conversations are varied and often. The child's interest can be paramount so there needs to be no conflict between agenda and preference. Being intrinsically motivated, the learner optimises learning by having control over what is learnt, when and where it is learnt, how it is learnt. Consent is foundational to the whole learning process. Resources can be precisely tailored to the individual child or children so that even in the more financially challenged families, the resources that exist will be just the ones that serve their needs.

Not only does home education overcome the inefficiencies of attempting to teach children unwanted material without their consent, it allows for a much broader definition of resources. The resources that are most suited to a process of conjecture and refutation and genuine growth of knowledge are much more readily available outside of schools. What are these resources?

Firstly, **conversation**: Both Alan Thomas and Roland Meighan, in their studies of home-based education, have concluded that an enormous amount of learning takes place through informal, but highly purposeful conversation. (cf. Alan Thomas, *Educating Children At Home* and Roland Meighan, *The Next Learning System*). This fundamental and powerful educational tool is not something that can be pre-planned. It is something that engaged and interactive homes are ideally suited to. It is also a resource that can be constructively expanded by bringing others into the conversation. As we have already seen, this is exactly what David Albert describes in his book, *And the Skylark Sings with Me.* Conversations with his children may sometimes have reached points where the conjectures needed more input than he could give and so experts were approached; not teachers, but real practitioners with a passion to share. Sometimes these conversations will involve highly practical interactions, as we saw with Julia Bergson-Shilcock's regular visits to a veterinary surgery, or as might be the case where the ideas are about music or learning to drive or woodwork. Conversation; with amateurs, with professionals, with peers, with practitioners, with those who are simply interested enough to share idea, are perhaps the most powerful learning resource we have. Access to such conversations is a strong feature of home education.

Secondly, **communication media**: The push for computers in schools can rarely rival the availability of modern communication tools in the homes of those who make a conscious decision to exploit these facilities to the fullest. The Internet has opened up a learning resource that would have looked like magic only twenty years ago. With progressively cheaper telephone lines and Internet access, home-educated children are ideally placed to use the resources offered by computer technology more fully than their school-going peers. Furthermore, they can access the sites and information that interests them, that contributes to their own conjectures, that feeds their intrinsic motivation. Whilst schools concentrate on 'educational' software and 'educational' websites, home-educated children can use a much fuller range of resources, including computer games, which David Deutsch has described as 'a unique educational environment'.

> *"They provide a unique learning environment. They provide something which for most of human history was not available, namely, an interactive complex entity that is accessible at low cost and zero risk.*

> *"Let's compare video games with other great educational things in the world. Books and television have great complexity and diversity - they give you access to almost every aspect of human culture and knowledge - but they are not interactive. On the other hand, something like playing the piano is also complex, and interactive, but it requires an enormous initial investment (months or years of practice or training) with the associated huge risk of misplacing that investment. One cannot make many such investments in one's life. ....*

> *"Apart from conversation, all the complex interactive things require a huge initial investment, except video games, and I think video games are a breakthrough in human culture for that reason. They are not some transient, fringe aspect of culture; they are destined to be an important means of human learning for the rest of history, because of this interactive element. Why is being interactive so important? Because interacting with a complex entity is what life and thinking and creativity and art and science are all about."*
> (Deutsch, David, *Video Games: Harmfully addictive or Unique Educational Environment*)

With the increasing availability of websites where players can engage in multiplayer computer games from disparate locations around the world, this complexity and interactivity continues to escalate. Without the constraints of school timetables and the enforced 'bedtimes' that tend to go with getting up for school, home-educated children are well placed to take advantage of these complex, interactive, unique learning environments. Internet communication, which gives access to specialised global discussion groups, chat rooms for every conceivable interest, a burgeoning plethora of websites available at any time in any location, and complex, interactive computer games explored alone or in virtual groups, are available to anyone, but home-educated children have much less pressure on their time and availability.

The same is true of access to television with its information and cultural richness. I recently heard a teacher asking a home-educated child what she had learnt at 'home-school' this year. *"I know just about the whole script of the first three series of 'Friends'"*, the twelve-year-old replied. The teacher was not amused, but it was in fact an excellent answer. The girl had stayed up late for many nights watching the same episodes over and over again, following them up with website searches and increasingly complex conversations about the cultural material being presented in such a digestible form. The learning that took place was immeasurable, and sparked off other avenues of interest, exploration, conjecture and refutation.

Not all home educating families are equally positive about the educational opportunities of computers, computer games, television and videos. Some take an anti-technology stance and severely limit or entirely forbid the use of some or all of these resources. It is home education, however, that potentially allows maximum exploitation of these resources. Freed from the constraints of early nights and timetables, home education affords an unrivalled opportunity to explore as much or as little as intrinsic motivation prompts.

Thirdly, **the real world**: I have an abhorrence of the phrase 'the real world'; it is a convenient fiction coined to put down any experience or activity that someone wants to demean out of hand. It is often used against home educators; 'children should learn to cope with the real world' (i.e.school); 'you can't protect your children from the real world forever' (implying that home education is a form of over-protective fearfulness on our children's behalf). In fact, we all live in the real world, there is no other world to live in. In that real world, there are many resources that can be dipped into or explored more fully. Home-educated children have the time to do this as the motivation takes them. A home-educated child does not have to wait for a two week, second best work experience placement at the end of their school career to be able to sample different work environments or special areas of interest. The home-educated child does not have to explore a museum with a clipboard in hand ticking off the right boxes on the once-only trip. She/he can explore at her/his leisure, visit only the parts that attract her, return when she wants to, ask the questions she wants answers to, without being derided by peers or urged by harassed teachers to get on the coach now. The home-educated child can use the library whenever it is appropriate to her/his learning objectives, not only during the once-a-month library visit when she/he has to listen to convoluted explanations of how a library works and take out only the books that are in the right area. The home-educated child chooses concert and theatre trips that attract him, not those that happen to offer cheap tickets for 'educational' performances. She can go to the cinema on weekdays when it is quiet, swim when the pools are virtually empty, learn for herself how to shop and cook.

The notion of mentors has recently entered the school system in the form of role models who will urge black children or male children (or whatever group are perceived as failing) to make the most of their 'education'. This is a far cry from the Albert family's use of mentors; passionate practitioners who want to share their ideas with people of any age who are interested. We all live in the real world and, far from being protected from it, home-educated children have the potential to utilise the resources of that world to real benefit.

Fourthly, **books**: Schools have books, but they are not the books that the children have chosen. Rather, the emphasis is on functional literacy at particular ages and stages in place of unfettered exploration for its own sake. Literacy is an interesting concept. In schools it is essential that children can read at earlier and earlier ages, because literacy facilitates the teaching methodology and aids control. Many home-educated children learn to 'read' at much later ages, and yet have a love affair with books long before they are literate (by school definitions) and continue this passion once they acquire literacy for their own ends. (cf, research findings of Meighan, Thomas and Rothermel).

The books that home-educated children use are not those that are prescribed, but a vast array reflecting the diversity of interest of the children. Moreover, this diversity often becomes a family trait, swelling the learning that is taking place, as Terri Dowty says:

> "Ian and I owe our revived enthusiasm for life to (the children)...It is their example which has taken me to the 'new non-fiction' shelves of the bookshop and made me bring home books about William Morris, Tibet and global economics. Thanks to them I am willing to try anything...."
> (Dowty, Terri, 'Lessons from the leg-break fairy', in *Free Range Education*, p.62)

Fifthly, home education is best placed to utilise a selection of **bespoke resources**: A tailor-made education will involve tailor-made resources. The nine-year-old harpist, the ten-year-old jeweller, the thirteen-year-old carpenter, the eight-year-old ornithologist each require resources that are particular to that child's interests at that time. Schools can cater only for the most general interests; percussion instruments, general tools and art supplies, often in short supply. Specialisms have to be pursued elsewhere, in the precious few hours after homework and before bed or during highly pressurised weekends. Home-educated children have no such constraints; the home educated-child can spend a fortnight on one sculpture, a month composing a piece of music, weeks working on a website. The resources follow the child, not the child the available resources.

Home education makes full use of a culture of resources: conversation, communication media, the community and world at large, books and specialist resources form a network of learning opportunities that are maximised by intrinsic motivation. No other education can be so efficient.

Event-driven living, event-driven learning
Society is increasingly postmodern. This is a complex notion, but amongst other features Mary Klages has defined postmodernism as, like modernism:

> *"rejecting boundaries between high and low forms of art, rejecting rigid genre distinctions, emphasizing pastiche, parody, bricolage, irony, and playfulness...."*

It is, however, unlike modernism in that it:

> *"...doesn't lament the idea of fragmentation, provisionality, or incoherence, but rather celebrates that....*

> *"Another way of looking at...postmodernism are cultural formations which accompany particular stages of capitalism...The third, the phase we're in now, is multinational or consumer capitalism (with the emphasis placed on marketing, selling, and consuming commodities, not on producing them) associated with nuclear and electronic technologies, and correlated with postmodernism...*

> *"Modernity is fundamentally about order: ...creating order out of chaos. The assumption is...that the more ordered a society is, the better it will function...Because modernity is about the pursuit of ever-increasing levels of order, modern*

societies constantly are on guard against anything and everything labelled as 'disorder', which might disrupt order. Thus modern societies rely on continually establishing a binary opposition between 'order' and 'disorder', so that they can assert the superiority of 'order'. But to do this, they have to have things that represent 'disorder' - modern societies thus continually have to create/construct 'disorder'. In western culture, this disorder becomes 'the other' - defined in relation to other binary oppositions. Thus anything non-white, non-male, non-heterosexual, non-hygienic...becomes part of 'disorder', and has to be eliminated from the ordered...society.

"...Totality, and stability, and order, Lyotard argues, are maintained in modern societies through the means of 'grand narratives' or 'master narratives', which are stories a culture tells itself about its practices and beliefs.

"...Postmodernism then is the critique of grand narratives, the awareness that such narratives serve to mask the contradictions and instabilities that are inherent in any social organization or practice...

"...Finally, postmodernism is concerned with questions of the organization of knowledge.... In a postmodern society, however, knowledge becomes functional--you learn things, not to know them, but to use that knowledge.

"...Not only is knowledge in postmodern societies characterized by its utility, but knowledge is also distributed, stored, and arranged differently in postmodern societies than in modern ones. Specifically, the advent of electronic computer technologies has revolutionized the modes of knowledge production, distribution, and consumption in our society (indeed, some might argue that postmodernism is best described by, and correlated with, the emergence of computer technology, starting in the 1960s, as the dominant force in all aspects of social life).
(Klages, Mary, *Post Modernism*, December 3, 1997)

Home education is at the cutting edge of postmodernism. It enables people to define community in terms of a specific interest group; it maximises diversity and flexibility; it includes scope for utilising the full range of electronic media; it allows learners to access the knowledge that is most useful to them; it allows families scope to adopt every conceivable lifestyle; it is comfortable with constant change. While manufacturing, shopping, leisure, entertainment, commerce and services increasingly become twenty-four hour, seven day a week activities accessed on an event-driven, flexible basis, schools persist with a narrow 'nine-till-three weekday', definition of learning that is increasingly at odds with the world.

This is not to say that postmodernism is the last word in culture. Its realisation that solutions have to be held tentatively, for example, does not justify its common assumption that there may be no such thing as truth. We do not have to slide fallibility and tentatively held knowledge into moral relativism. We can still hold that knowledge for its own sake is itself a worthwhile enough utility to an autonomous individual. None-the-less, home-educated children are most likely to be in a position to take their place in a society of event-driven living and learning, particularly if they are educated autonomously and are used to meeting their preferences and finding solutions - as children who come from TCS homes would be.

Cheap at the price

Home education undoubtedly has costs, but there is no such thing as free education. We have to decide what costs we are willing to pay. For some families this will be a particularly hard decision, but the range of creative solutions across every kind of family of every level of income and lifestyle are an enormous testimony to the possibility of home education for anyone. One home educator writes:

> "In our family I gave up teaching in order to home educate...

> "We do miss the money and it would obviously be great to have that extra £17,000 + a year. But we have made the conscious decision as a family to have less money in order for me to be with the children.

> "(My husband) does a job...which he doesn't like doing at all, the pay is poor...The one advantage is that he works shifts so he can often come to activities in the day which he couldn't do if he worked a regular day job...."

Many parents are prepared to make enormous sacrifices. Many see the lower incomes not as sacrifices, but as real preferences in order to be doing what really matters to the whole family. Many parents, including single parents, find increasingly innovative ways to both make a living and home educate. Some home educators would gladly accept government finance for their educational choices if it were available. Others rightly point out that funding and control go hand in hand. We cannot expect the government to commit taxpayers' money to private education carried out within families without also expecting intrusive and narrowing definitions of what that education should look like.

Living without state funding in education is not an easy choice for many families, but the financial costs assume a much lesser significance when they are compared to the high costs of compulsory, free education. Once school becomes compulsory, the potential costs of coercion to any individual child can escalate continually. In comparison to this, home education is certainly cheap at the price.

Bound to be 'free'

'Free' is a slippery word. Financially, no education is free. If it is provided by the state, then the cost is paid by the taxpayer and for some, this fact alone involves an immoral level of coercion. Whatever our political stance on funding by taxation, tax-funded education must be accountable to the policies of the day, and these policies will be paramount over the needs of individual children. Any education that is free at the point of delivery is bound to be a means of social engineering as much as it is a means of attempting to deliver education. This is clearly demonstrated in the way in which education involves itself with ensuring conformity, even when this means subjecting children to demeaning labels, diagnosing, medicating and treating them, or even when this involves labelling whole families as dysfunctional or bad and subjecting them to wholesale behaviour modification in the form of therapy.

Home education allows the possibility of throwing off the bindings of compulsory state schooling in favour of 'freedom' - the chance for children to learn what they want, when they want, how they want. It is a chance that not all home educators take; some, believing that it is parents and not the state that are the best arbiters of their children's best interests, will replace one authority by another. Even in these cases, however, there is likely to be more flexibility in how children learn and how they contribute to their own education, simply as a result of accessing the resources of purposive conversation and individualised learning environments. For children whose autonomy is respected and nurtured, home education allows intrinsic motivation to be paramount and for minds to roam free.

Home education, particularly when it is combined with recognition of children's autonomy, also has the interesting spin-off of 'freeing' parents. This is not simply in the obvious ways of not having to live lives around a 'nine till three' day organized in rigid terms and not being subject to outside intrusion and judgments. In the process of respecting and nurturing our children's autonomy, the unexpected benefits of continuing learning and education for the parents often becomes every bit as important as children's education. Home education is a continuing adventure for the entire family, opening up new areas of interest for adults and children alike (as Terri Dowty notes in the quote above) and often challenging families constantly to re-appraise how they live together, how they use space and resources, how they make a living, how they connect with the world.   Home education is not monetarily free, but it loses the bindings that limit our freedom to follow intrinsic motivations and spend a lifetime making new knowledge. Home education provides an arena where parents and children alike can satisfy their preferences and find the solutions they seek.

References and further reading

Albert, D. (1999) 'And the Skylark Sings with Me', in *Growing Without Schooling*, New Society Publishers, issue 130

Ashford, N. (1993) *Dismantling the Welfare State: why and how*, Political Notes 86, occasional paper for Libertarian Alliance

Barkley R. 'ADHD' in *Scientific American* available at www.sciam.com

Baughaman F.A. (2000) *Still Seeking ADHD*, paper Americana Anthropological Association

Baxter, R., *Public School Pandemonium: my experience as a public school teacher* at: http://www.lp.org/lpnews/0102/schools.html

Bergson-Shilcock, A., 'Grades Cause Problems, Get in the Way of Learning', first published in *The Daily Pennsylvanian*, quoted in Growing Without Schooling, issue 129

Bergson-Shilcock, J. 'Observing Veterinary Surgery; Breeding Cats', *Growing Without Schooling*, issue 131

Blankertz, S.(1991)*'The Manufacture of Subjection: A Critique of Compulsory State Education'*, Rotterdam

Crime and Disorder Act Guidance document at: www.homeoffice.gov.uk/cdact/truancy/htm

Dawkins, R. (1989) *The Selfish Gene*, Oxford Paperbacks

Day, K. (2000) 'What Lloyd Did Next', in *Free Range Education*, Stroud: Hawthorn Press

Deutsch, D. (1998) 'Education For Greatness', TCS Journal 27

Deutsch, D. (1999) TCS mailing list. archives at: www.tcs.ac

Deutsch, D. (2000) 'Anna's Story', TCS mailing list archives at: www.tcs.ac

Dowty, I. (2000) 'An Outline of the Law and Practice of Home-Based Education', in *Free Range Education*, edited Dowty, T., Stroud: Hawthorn Press

Dowty, T. 'Lessons from the leg-break fairy', in *Free Range Education*, edited Dowty,T., Stroud: Hawthorn Press

Falbel, A., 'Growing Without Education' in *Growing Without Schooling*, issue 130

Fortune-Wood, J. (2000) *Doing It Their Way: home-based education and autonomous learning*, Nottingham: Educational Heretics Press

Fortune-Wood, J. (2000) *Without Boundaries: consent-based, non-coercive parenting and autonomous learning*, Nottingham: Educational Heretics Press

Fortune-Wood, J. (2001) 'Living Without the Label' in *Paths are Made By Walking*, edited Dowty, T & Cowlishaw, K., London: Jessica Kingsley Publishers

Fortune-Wood, M.C. (November 2000) *School Phobia* article at: http://www.home-education.org.uk

Fortune-Wood, M.C., first published in Education Otherwise at: http://www.home-education.org.uk

Fortune-Wood, M.C., *Homeschooling Alone*, at: http://www.home-education.org.uk

Fortune-Wood, T. (23.01.01) letter to *The Guardian*

Gatto, J.T. (1991) 'The Six-Lesson Schoolteacher', *in Whole Earth Review*, Fall issue

Gibran, K. (1996) *The Prophet*; Wordsworth Editions Ltd

Holt, J. (1982) *Teach Your Own*, Diss: Lighthouse Books

Holt, J. (1977) *Instead of Education*, Harmondsworth: Penguin

Klages, M., *Post Modernism*, December 3, 1997 at: www.colorado.edu/English/ENGL2012klages/pomo.html

Lawrence, S. (1992) Extracts from TCS website copyright TCS, 'Video Games: Harmfully Addictive or a Unique Educational Environment?' by David Deustsch. The website article is a slightly modified version of a 1992 article from *Taking Children Seriously* issue 4, 'An interview with David Deutsch,' by Sarah Lawrence

Meighan, R. (1997) *The Next Learning System*, Nottingham: Educational Heretics Press

Popper, K. (1995) *The Myth of the Framework*, Routledge

Rothermel P.(1998) *Home Education: a critical evaluation,* Paper presented at the British Psychological Society Annual Education Conference, University of Exeter

Ruenzel, D. (March 2001) *The World According To Gatto,* Teacher Magazine at: www.teachermagazine.org/tm/tmstory.cfm?slug=06gatto.h12

Social Exclusion Unit (May 1998) *Truancy and School Exclusion,* Report at: www.cabinet-office.gov.uk

Suprinovicz, V. 'Educrats Declare War on Remaining Parental Rights.' Mountain Media: the Libertarian (2001) posted to the TCS list, March 14th 2001

Szasz, T. (March 1998) Thomas S. Szasz Cybercenter for Liberty and Responsibility

Szasz, T. 'Chemical Straitjackets for Children', *Ideas on Liberty,* 50: 38-39 (July), 2000. Sheldon Richman, Editor, *Ideas on Liberty* published by The Foundation for Economic Education, New York

Thomas, A. (2000) *Educating Children At Home, London:* Continuum.

Tomasevski, K. (1998 –1999) United Nations Special Rapporteur on the right to education, submitted in accordance with the Commission on Human Rights Resolution 1998/33 United Nations Commission on Human Rights & Statement on the Right to Education 8/4/99

Webb, J. (1999) *Those Unschooled Minds,* Nottingham: Educational Heretics Press

Wyatt, R.C., Interview with Thomas Szasz, www.psychotheraopistresources.com